THE CRIMINAL COURTS OF THE ROMAN REPUBLIC AND PRINCIPATE

BY THE SAME AUTHOR

Sparta

Athenian Democracy

The Later Roman Empire

Studies in Roman Government and Law

THE CRIMINAL COURTS OF THE ROMAN REPUBLIC AND PRINCIPATE

A. H. M. JONES

With a Preface by

JOHN CROOK

1972

BASIL BLACKWELL · OXFORD

ISBN 0 631 13900 1

Library of Congress Catalog Card Number:
75–149148

PRINTED IN GREAT BRITAIN
BY A. T. BROOME AND SON, 18 ST. CLEMENT'S, OXFORD
AND BOUND BY THE KEMP HALL BINDERY, OXFORD

PREFACE

Not many weeks before his death the late Professor A. H. M. Jones brought me the substantial manuscript which is here published, and we considered a date when we might discuss some points in it. Our intention had for some time been to publish a joint work on the Roman courts of justice, in which Professor Jones would deal with the criminal courts and I with the civil, and we had already had a number of discussions of earlier drafts of his half of the joint work. Now that he is dead I believe that what he had to say about the criminal courts is too important to be doomed to wait upon my dubious gropings on the civil side and can—and so here does—stand on its own.

The manuscript was complete, down to the notes, but it was still a draft, which Professor Jones would have worked over in the light of our further discussions and tidied up. It is here printed very nearly exactly as he wrote it. I have not presumed to alter its content of statements of fact and judgments in any way, except tacitly to correct two or three small errors; where, here and there, I do not agree with Professor Jones's argument or conclusions, and think it possible that he might have altered or re-worded them upon discussion, I have nevertheless refrained from making any such modifications myself. The paragraphing, the phraseology somewhat, and in some details but no major feature the arrangement of the material (when, for example, there were stray pieces of draft not yet clearly assigned to a specific point in the argument) I have manœuvred as seemed best and as I hope he would have liked; I do not think that anyone familiar with his work will feel that his characteristic voice has been blurred.

The third chapter inevitably retraces a certain amount of ground gone over before in some of the *Studies in Roman Government and Law*; but the subject is here, as it was not in those essays, seen as a whole. The work also ends abruptly, with no such summing up or general judgment on Roman criminal justice as Professor Jones would certainly have added to it; I have made no attempt to round it off with any substitute of mine.

One further thing it is appropriate to say: Professor Jones held very forcibly the belief that the only way to approach a historical subject without prejudice is to read the sources and make up one's mind on the basis of what they say. Apart from the *Untersuchungen zur Entwicklung des römischen Kriminalverfahrens in vorsullanischer Zeit* of Professor W. Kunkel, to which Chapter 1 of this work was expressly intended as a counterpoise, the reader will find virtually no reference to the views of other scholars about any of the numerous problems which the subject generates. It must not be held to follow that Professor Jones did not know those other views; but he quite deliberately put them out of consideration in order to concentrate the laser of his lucid mind on the primary evidence. I am convinced that, even if it may sometimes be disappointing not to know how he would have dealt with this or that important theory about Roman constitutional antiquities, the work here published stands nevertheless as a classic example of what can be achieved by the single eye, the steady, undiverted gaze.

My pupils Carolyn Brydon and Stephen Sugden have done Professor Jones's memory great service by helping me with the proofs.

JOHN CROOK.

CONTENTS

Chapter I

IUDICIA POPULI

CICERO and, it would seem, the annalists of his age from whom Livy and Dionysius of Halicarnassus and the collectors of anecdotes like Valerius Maximus and Aulus Gellius drew their material, believed that from the beginning of the Roman Republic until the establishment of the *iudicia publica* all crimes, whether political or ordinary offences such as murder, were normally tried by a *iudicium populi* if the penalty was death or scourging or a fine above a certain limit. This procedure arose, they believed, from the right of *provocatio ad populum* first enacted in 509 B.C. The rule was that a magistrate, after conducting preliminary investigations in public, gave sentence, and that the accused, if condemned, appealed to the people, and the assembly, after further argument, confirmed or rejected the magistrate's sentence. The only exceptions to this procedure were that a dictator in early times was not subject to *provocatio* (it is nowhere stated when he became subject), and that on special occasions the people might by a law empower one or more of the higher magistrates (the consuls or praetors) to exercise criminal jurisdiction; the choice of the magistrate was often left to the senate. Sometimes also the senate took such action without authorization by the people, but the legality of such a step was questioned.

This belief of Cicero and his contemporaries has been in modern times challenged in two ways. It has in the first place been argued that *provocatio* played no part in a *iudicium populi*, that the magistrate did not condemn the accused who then appealed, but put the issue of guilty or not guilty to the assembly.[1] More recently it has been argued that *iudicia populi* were held only on political charges brought by the tribunes of the plebs, and that ordinary crimes were tried by a praetor, or in minor cases a *triumvir capitalis*, sitting with assessors, and that there was no appeal from such a sentence.[2]

On the early procedure for criminal trials, as on all questions of early Roman history, some scepticism is justifiable. The most scientific method is to proceed from the known to the unknown, to reconstruct as far as possible the procedure of criminal trials in the historical period, say from the middle of the third century B.C. It may then be possible to argue back to the earlier period.

To the evidence of what actually happened in criminal trials of the last two centuries of the Republic may be added that of Cicero in the *de legibus*. The constitution which he describes in that work is, it is true, an ideal constitution, but it is in the main the Roman constitution of what Cicero regarded as the best period, the early second century B.C. There are certain archaic features. The dictatorship, which had for practical purposes been obsolete since 216 B.C., is re-introduced;[3] it may be that Cicero by the end of his life saw the weaknesses of the *senatus consultum ultimum*, which had been invented to replace the dictatorship in dealing with serious civil disturbances. *Provocatio* is not allowed *militiae*,[4] though it had apparently been granted at some time in the first half of the second century B.C. On the other hand one of Sulla's innovations is approved, that the senate should not be chosen by the censors but automatically recruited from ex-magistrates; this is emphasised in the following discussion.[5] There are also a few improvements invented by Cicero: the abolition of *liberae legationes*, the censorial function of keeping true copies of laws, the mixed system of open and secret ballot; all are commented upon in the discussion.[6]

The constitution, though described with enigmatic brevity, is meant to be complete: in the discussion the brief enactments of the code are explained and amplified, but no new provisions are introduced. All that Cicero has to say on the administration of justice is therefore in the text of the constitution, and if there was a discussion of the question in a part of the dialogue now lost, it could only have explained and justified the rules in the text. Now the *iudicia publica* of the later Republic do not here appear (and the chief praetor has charge of civil jurisdiction only,[7] while the functions of his colleagues are unspecified). What is laid down is as follows:

'Magistratus nec oboedientem et noxium civem multa, vinculis verberibusve coerceto, ni par maiorve potestas populusve prohibessit, ad quos provocatio esto. cum magistratus iudicassit inrogassitve, per populum multae poenae certatio esto.'[8]

This may refer primarily to the *coercitio* by a magistrate of a citizen who defies his lawful orders. This is suggested by the absence of the death penalty, which certainly was enacted by the laws for certain crimes in Cicero's ideal republic, and by the presence of imprisonment and flogging, which were not penalties for crime. But it would seem to cover minor breaches of the laws: the accused include not only the disobedient but the *noxii*, who must surely be those guilty of a legal offence. The other passages referring to criminal jurisdiction are: 'omnes magistratus auspicium iudiciumque habento', the inclusion of *iudicia* among the functions of the assembly, and the provision 'de capite civis nisi per maximum comitiatum . . . ne ferunto',[9] together with commentary on the first passage:

'deinceps igitur omnibus magistratibus auspicia et iudicia dantur: iudicia, ut esset populi potestas ad quam provocaretur.'[10] It is clear that in all criminal cases, as in cases of disobedience to the magistrates, the procedure was the same: the magistrate pronounced judgment, the condemned appealed, and the people decided by their vote. In fact the only form of criminal trial was the *iudicium populi*.

It may seem a surprisingly retrograde suggestion of Cicero's to abolish the *iudicia publica*, which in the eyes of modern historians are regarded as a great advance in the history of Roman criminal justice. But Cicero had plenty of experience of the venality of the juries in the *iudicia publica*, and may well have thought that the old system of popular trials would be less liable to that evil; and it should be remembered that capital trials would in his ideal republic, as in the actual Republic of the earlier second century B.C., have come before the *comitia centuriata*, where 'good men' controlled the vote. It may be noted that a contemporary of Cicero, whether he be Sallust or not, was also so deeply dissatisfied with the corruption of the juries as constituted in his day that he proposed larger juries, for which all citizens of the first class should be eligible, remarking that Rhodes and other Greek cities found large juries chosen by lot from rich and poor alike very satisfactory.[11] However that may be, it is certain that Cicero proposed that all crimes should be tried in *iudicia populi* and also certain that in doing so he thought he was reviving the practice of the good old days before the *iudicia publica* were established. It seems unlikely that he can have been so grossly deceived in this as some modern critics believe.

On the procedure of *iudicia populi* Cicero cannot possibly have been ignorant. In Cicero's childhood and youth there was a great spate of popular trials. In 106, the year of his birth, C. Caelius, tribune of the plebs, prosecuted and convicted C. Popilius Laenas for *perduellio*.[12] It was a celebrated case, for two reasons: voting was by ballot for the first time, under a law passed for the purpose by the accusing tribune, and the legal argument was interesting and became a stock theme in rhetorical handbooks: was Laenas, legate of Cassius Longinus, guilty of *perduellio* in saving the Roman army by surrendering its arms? In 104 Cn. Domitius, tribune of the plebs, unsuccessfully prosecuted M. Junius Silanus for making war on the Cimbri without orders from the people (this was also presumably *perduellio*),[13] and also M. Aemilius Scaurus, for a fine, 'quod eius opera sacra populi Romani deminuta esse diceret'.[14] In 103 Q. Servilius Caepio (cos. 106) and Cn. Mallius Maximus (cos. 105) were prosecuted and convicted by the tribunes for their defeat by the Cimbri in 105.[15] In 100 Metellus Numidicus was successfully prosecuted by Saturninus, a tribune of the plebs, for refusing to take the oath prescribed by the latter's agrarian law.[16] In 98 C. Appuleius Decianus accused L. Valerius Flaccus, curule aedile of the previous year.[17] He also accused P. Furius, a tribune of the previous year, for opposing Metellus' recall;[18] he failed to secure a conviction, but one of his colleagues, C. Canuleius, brought the same charge against Furius, who was lynched by the assembly.[19] In 87–6 a number of persons were accused before the people: Sulla by M. Vergilius, tribune of the plebs, Mucius Scaevola by Fimbria (office not stated), Cornelius Merula and Lutatius Catulus (accusers unknown), and nine tribunes by the remaining tribune.[20] By this time Cicero was almost twenty years of age.

After this *iudicia populi* were much rarer, but some occurred in

Cicero's mature years. The first case is dubious: in 66 C. Memmius, probably tribune of the plebs (though this is nowhere stated), prosecuted M. Lucullus for his conduct as quaestor (or legate) of Sulla in 83;[21] but this may have been before a jury court, as a tribune could perfectly well bring an action in a *iudicium publicum*. In 63 C. Rabirius was tried before the *comitia centuriata* by *duoviri perduellionis*, and—when the trial was stopped by Cicero as consul—by Labienus, tribune of the plebs, probably also before the *comitia centuriata* for *perduellio*; Cicero defended him at this second trial.[22] Caesar in 58, when leaving for his province, was accused by L. Antistius, tribune of the plebs, but persuaded the other tribunes to stop the trial on the ground that he was absent on public business.[23] If the case had been for trial in a *iudicium publicum* the veto would not have served to stop it, and further Caesar could have legally claimed exemption as a matter of course as being *reipublicae causa absens*. The proposed trial was therefore probably to be before the people, in which case the tribunes were not bound by any such rule.[24] On this second ground the contemporary judicial attack on Caesar's quaestor must also have been by a *iudicium populi*. In 56 B.C. Clodius, as curule aedile, accused Milo before the people *de vi*;[25] Cicero attended the first two sessions and described them in letters to his brother.[26] Finally in 43 two tribunes accused a man for greeting Caesar as king; their joint accusation suggests a *iudicium populi*.[27] It may also be remarked that Cicero himself in 70 B.C. threatened to accuse any corrupt jurors in the Verres case, and Verres himself, before the people next year, when he would be aedile,[28] and Clodius as aedile in 56 threatened to prosecute Cicero before the people.[29]

These are political cases, nearly all brought by tribunes of the plebs, one brought and two threatened by aediles. Only two *iudicia populi* for ordinary crimes are attested in Cicero's lifetime. In a year between 105 and 102 in his narrative Orosius, presumably copying Livy, states that 'Q. Fabius Maximus killed his own young son, whom he had banished to the country, with the aid of two slaves as agents of the murder, and forthwith freed the slaves as the reward of their crime. A day being named, Cn. Pompeius being the accuser, he was condemned (die dicta Cn. Pompeio accusante damnatus est)'.[30] *Diem dicere* is the technical term for initiating a *iudicium populi*, and is exclusive to it. Cn. Pompeius was quaestor in 104 or 103.[31] It is difficult to resist the suggestion that this trial was the last recorded case of the traditional procedure alluded to by the antiquarians, where *quaestores parricidii* accused for murder before the *comitia centuriata*. The other case is recorded by Valerius Maximus. He states that Metellus Celer accused and convicted before the people ('diem ad populum dicente') one Cn. Sergius Silus of attempting to bribe a married woman to commit adultery with him.[32] The date is uncertain: the elder Metellus Celer was tribune of the plebs in 90, the younger perhaps in 72 or 68; both may be presumed to have been aediles a year or two later.[33] The charge of *stuprum* was normally handled in historical times by the aediles, but the tribunes are said to have acted in two cases in the late fourth century or early third. Cicero may, then, have been a middle-aged man at the time of the adultery case, or in his late teens. He could have heard accounts of the murder case, which was evidently a *cause célèbre*, since it got into history books, from his older contemporaries.

Cicero briefly describes the procedure of a *iudicium populi* in the following words:

> 'Nam cum tam moderata iudicia populi sint a maioribus constituta, primum ut ne poena capitis cum pecunia coniungatur, deinde ne nisi prodicta die quis accusetur, ut ter ante magistratus accuset intermissa die quam multam inroget aut iudicet, quarta sit accusatio trinum nundinum prodicta die, quo die iudicium sit futurum. . . .'[34]

The general outline is clear. First came the notice of trial. Then three sessions at intervals of (at least) one day, at which the magistrate investigated the case, then after an interval of (at least) a *trinum nundinum* the formal judgment of the magistrate and the vote of the people. This general picture is borne out by the descriptions of trials, but the details of the procedure are obscure, partly because most of the accounts are condensed and often somewhat confused, partly because the technical terms are often loosely used. It may be also that the procedure was somewhat fluid.

At the first step, universally described as *diem dicere*, the magistrate fixed a day on which the trial could begin, named the accused, and also apparently specified the charge or charges and the penalty. In the narratives of the trials the charge is often implicitly given in the preceding narrative, when it is sometimes mixed with the accuser's motive, or is developed in the story of the trial. In a number of cases, however, it is linked with *dictio diei* in what looks like official language. In the trial of Acilius Glabrio in 189, for instance, 'P. Sempronius Gracchus et C. Sempronius Rutilus tribuni plebis ei diem dixerunt quod pecuniae regiae praedaeque aliquantum captae in Antiochi castris neque in triumpho tulisset neque in aerarium rettulisset'.[35] In the trial of the two censors in 169 the tribune P. Rutilius 'C. Claudio diem dixit quod contionem ab se avocasset',[36] and in 104 B.C. Cn. Domitius, tribune of the plebs, 'diem ei (Aemilio Scauro) dixit apud populum et multam irrogavit quod eius opera sacra populi Romani deminuta esse diceret'.[37] The penalty is often mentioned during or at the conclusion of the trial, but is sometimes recorded at the *diei dictio*. At the trial of the *publicanus* Postumius in 212 the narrative opens with the statement that the two tribunes Sp. and L. Carvilius 'ducentum milium aeris multam M. Postumio dixerunt'.[38] In the trial of Glabrio the penalty is not mentioned at the *diei dictio*, but in the description of the trial it is stated that 'centum milium multa irrogata erat; bis de ea certatum est'.[39] The fine had been fixed before the trial began, presumably when the tribunes declared the day. On the other hand in the case of C. Lucretius in 171 two tribunes *diem dixerunt* and then 'C. Lucretium, ubi dies quae dicta erat venit, tribuni ad populum accusarunt, multamque deciens centum milium aeris dixerunt.'[40] Had they named no figure initially, or did they alter the figure during the trial (see below), or is Livy being inaccurate? These are all cases of fines, but if the magistrate intended to inflict a capital sentence he might apparently express it in two ways. In the second trial of Postumius the *publicanus* the tribunes 'rei capitalis diem Postumio dixerunt'.[41] In the trial of Claudius in 248 'dies ei dicta est perduellionis a Pullio et Fundanio tr. pl.'.[42] In the trial of the censors in 169, 'in ante dies octavum et septimum Kal. Octobres comitiis perduellionis dicta dies',[43] and on another occasion (the accused is unknown and the date uncertain but probably in the late second or early first century) 'Licinius tribunus plebi perduellionis ei diem dixit'.[44] If the charge fell within the category of *perduellio* it carried the death penalty.

The words used by the magistrate seem by Livy's reports in indirect speech to have been 'iudico perduellionis'. In 211 'tum Sempronius perduellionis se iudicare Cn. Fulvio dixit',[45] and in 169 the tribune 'utrique censori perduellionis se iudicare pronuntiavit'.[46] He also, it would seem, said 'multam irrogo' when he *diem dixit* for a fine. He did not actually *iudicare* or *multam irrogare* until the fourth session, when the vote was taken, as Cicero says; thus the present tense must have been used proleptically.

The magistrate might, and often did, include a number of charges in the same accusation, but he was not allowed to leave the penalty open. He had to name one penalty, death or a fine (apparently a stated sum) for the whole lot. This must be the meaning of Cicero's 'ut ne poena capitis cum pecunia coniungatur', for the magistrate could hardly sentence a man to death *plus* a fine of 10,000 asses. He could however change his mind about the penalty during the proceedings as late as the third session. The only recorded reduction (from death to a fine) is in the mythical period,[47] but there is a well attested case of the reverse change in 211. The tribune C. Sempronius Blaesus began with a fine when prosecuting the praetor Fulvius for cowardice in battle, but when evidence was given in the third session that he had actually initiated the flight of the army, the assembly shouted for the death penalty and the tribune acceded to their demand. An appeal was made to the other tribunes, but they declared that their colleague's action was *more maiorum*.[48] The tribune T. Labienus seems to have done the same in the case of Rabirius. He apparently started with a fine ('multae irrogatione') for a jumble of alleged offences: violation of sacred places, peculation and arson (the burning of the record office), murder of his nephew, harbouring of other persons' slaves, killing and flogging Roman citizens in Apulia, and unspecified sexual offences—it is not clear whether the murder of Saturninus figured on the original charge sheet. But by the stage of the trial at which Cicero spoke the charge was capital for *perduellio*.[49]

We have an eyewitness account of the first two sessions of Clodius' prosecution of Milo in 56 in two letters of Cicero to his brother.[50] The first was held on 2 Feb.; Milo duly appeared, and with him Pompey, described as his advocate. Marcellus spoke for the defence and no doubt Clodius and others on the other side. The next session was fixed for 6 Feb. On this day Milo again appeared and Pompey tried to speak but was howled down. When he had concluded Clodius tried to speak but was also howled down. A riot followed, and Clodius fixed the next meeting for 17 Feb. We are told nothing of this session nor of the fourth and final session which was fixed for 17 May. We also know that Vatinius gave evidence against Milo at this trial.[51]

The function of the magistrate who presided at these sessions is sometimes described as accusing (*accusare*), sometimes as investigating (*anquirere*).[52] He in fact is represented in the accounts as doing both. As at all *contiones*, he was in control and no one could speak unless invited by him; he could also limit the length of speeches, as Labienus did at the Rabirius trial.[53] He naturally and normally allowed the accused to speak and others to speak on his behalf.[54] He also called witnesses, who gave their evidence under oath.[55] The three sessions are mentioned at the trial of Fulvius in 211 and that of Acilius Glabrio in 189.[56] In the (perhaps fictitious) trial of Scipio Africanus described under the year 187 by Valerius Antias there are two sessions and notice of a third, which Scipio failed to attend, alleging ill-health.[57] Appian also mentions the four meetings (in all) in connection with trials in 87.[58]

On the fourth and final session our evidence is not plentiful. In the trial of Postumius the *publicanus*—where Livy says nothing of three previous sessions—the final speeches were made ('perorata causa'), presumably on both sides, witnesses were called ('testibus datis'), and the tribunes ordered the people to withdraw in order that the tribe in which the Latins should vote might be determined by lot and the vote might be taken.[59] In the trial of Claudius the censor—where again previous sessions are not mentioned—Claudius made his speech of defence ('causam dixit'), presumably in reply to a speech by the accusing tribune, and the people voted.[60] It would seem very unnecessary to repeat the whole trial, including the evidence, at the last session, and it may be that in these two cases the preliminary *contiones* had been omitted (see below), and that normally proceedings would have started with the formal judgment. No formal judgment by the accusing magistrate or *provocatio* by the accused is mentioned in either of these trials; but a formal judgment does appear to be mentioned in the case of L. Scipio in 187 B.C. as reported by Nepos. Here P. Scipio, in his appeal to the other tribunes on behalf of his brother, states that the tribune C. Minucius Augurinus, after disorderly proceedings, passed sentence upon him and imposed a fine and demanded sureties for its payment; *provocatio* and the vote of the people are omitted:

'Cum contra leges contraque morem maiorum tribunus pl. hominibus accitis per vim inauspicato sententiam de eo tulerit multamque nullo exemplo irrogaverit praedesque eum ob eam rem dare cogat . . .'[61]

Formal judgment followed by appeal is mentioned in the duumviral trial of Rabirius[62] and in the similar trial of Horatius,[63] which was doubtless the precedent cited for it *ex annalium monumentis atque ex regum commentariis*.[64] This may be bogus archaism, but it at least suggests that in the first century B.C. others besides Cicero believed that the *iudicium populi* was based on *provocatio*. There are three other recorded cases of *provocatio* in a popular trial, all against fines imposed by the *pontifex maximus*. One is in a passage of Festus so full of lacunae that little can be made of it. It appears to record a dispute on a fine point of sacred law between Metellus, *pontifex maximus* (there were three Metelli who held the office, in 243–21, 114–103 and 81–63) and a Claudius, in the course of which Claudius 'provocavit'.[65] The other two are clearer. In 189 the *pontifex maximus* P. Licinius forbade the *flamen Quirinalis* Q. Fabius Pictor, who had been elected praetor and allotted Sardinia, to proceed to his province, thereby abandoning his sacred duties. A great dispute followed and finally fines were imposed, an appeal made to the tribunes and *provocatio* to the people. In the end the *flamen* was ordered to be obedient to the *pontifex maximus*, but the fines were remitted by order of the people.[66] In 180 the *pontifex maximus* C. Servilius ordered the *duumvir navalis* L. Cornelius Dolabella to abdicate his office before being inaugurated as *rex sacrorum*. Dolabella refused and the *pontifex* imposed a fine on him; he appealed to the people, and they voted that they ordered the *duumvir* to obey the *pontifex*, the fine to be remitted if he duly abdicated. The voting was stopped by a storm.[67] A similar incident occurred in 131, when the consul and *pontifex maximus* Crassus ordered his fellow-consul Flaccus, *flamen Martialis*, not to proceed to Asia, and imposed a fine on him; no appeal is mentioned, but the people remitted the fine and ordered the *flamen* to obey the *pontifex*.[68]

There were—or could be—further speeches and argument after the *provocatio*. This is alleged to have happened in the duumviral trial of Horatius which served as a precedent for the first trial of Rabirius. In this case there was no argument *preceding* the formal judgment, nor apparently was there in Rabirius' case if Cicero is right in saying that he was condemned 'indicta causa' (after a speech of accusation by C. Julius Caesar, one of the *duoviri*, according to Suetonius). In Horatius' case the formula was 'si a duumviris provocarit, provocatione certato'. Horatius does appeal, and 'de provocatione certatum ad populum est', and Horatius' father, amongst others, makes a speech, after which the vote is taken.[69] Presumably it was intended that Rabirius' case should be argued after his appeal. Here again the procedure may be bogus archaism, but in the trials held by the *pontifices* some discussion must have intervened between the *provocatio* and the vote. In all cases the *pontifex* pronounced a fine, there was an appeal, and the people remitted the fine but ordered the accused to obey the *pontifex*. Now the assembly could only answer 'yes' or 'no' to a question put by the presiding magistrate. The *pontifex* must therefore have changed his proposal, and this implies that at the last moment the accused, seeing no doubt that the assembly was hostile, agreed to obey the *pontifex* and asked for the fine to be remitted, and the *pontifex* agreed to alter his motion accordingly.

It might perhaps be argued that *provocatio* was a peculiar feature of the jurisdiction of the *duoviri perduellionis* and the *pontifex maximus*; but there is no particular reason for thinking so. It is more likely that *provocatio* (and the antecedent judgment of the magistrate) are so rarely mentioned because we have so few descriptions of the final session of a *iudicium populi* and those we have are so brief. The important fact is that Cicero, who was certainly perfectly familiar with the procedure of a *iudicium populi*, when he described his ideal republic, which closely conformed to the usage of the second century, laid down the procedure as judgment by a magistrate, appeal, and vote of the people, for all criminal trials.

The voting at all trials for a fine was by a tribal assembly. Constitutional purists believe that where officers of the plebs, the tribunes and the plebeian aediles, were conducting the case the assembly was the *concilium plebis*, and when magistrates of the Roman people (that is, curule aediles and the *pontifex maximus*) were acting it was the *comitia populi tributa*; but in the historical period the two assemblies were in all essentials identical. Capital trials on the other hand in all recorded cases were decided by the *comitia centuriata*, in deference to a law of the Twelve Tables, often cited by Cicero.[70] The centuries are specifically mentioned in the cases of Claudius Pulcher in 241, the censor Claudius in 169, and Rabirius in 63 (probably at both trials); all these were for *perduellio*.[71] They are also mentioned in the 'commentarium vetus anquisitionis M'. Sergii M'. f. quaestoris qui capitis accusavit T. Quinctium Rocum', cited by Varro. The charge is unspecified and the date uncertain, except that it must fall after 243.[72] This meant that a tribune of the plebs, who had only the *ius agendi cum plebe*, had to ask a magistrate entitled to summon the *populus* (for all practical purposes a consul or praetor) 'for a day'. This procedure is attested three times, and in each case the urban praetor is asked. In 211 the tribune Sempronius, having at the third *contio* decided to make the charge capital, asked the urban praetor C. Calpurnius for a day for the *comitia*. In 169 Rutilius, starting his action for *perduellio* against the two censors, took the same step, and two consecutive days were named; he had shortly before declared a day for one censor, presumably for the first *contio*. Towards the end of the second century, or early in the first, the tribune Licinius stated the day for *perduellio* (for the first *contio*) and asked the urban praetor for a day for the *comitia*.[73] It must be presumed that the accusing tribune summoned and presided at the *comitia centuriata* (though this is nowhere made plain), having obtained auspices from the praetor. This is suggested by the procedure when the quaestors, who had no *ius agendi cum populo*, tried a capital case. According to the 'commentarium anquisitionis' mentioned above, one of the quaestors sent for the auspices to a praetor or consul but held the said auspices himself and instructed the herald to summon the *comitia* to him.[74] Curule aediles similarly had legally no *ius agendi cum populo*, nor plebeian aediles a *ius agendi cum plebe*, but they acquired it in practice by the same kind of ritual moves. Cicero indeed in two passages speaks as if he would in 69 as curule aedile have the *ius agendi cum populo* and would use it to prosecute corrupt jurors or Verres himself.[75] But this is not technical language, and in 56, speaking of a threatened trial of himself by Clodius as curule aedile, he says: 'diem dixisset, ut iecerat: fecissem ut ei statim tertius a praetore dies diceretur'.[76] The *pontifex maximus* and the *duoviri perduellionis* presumably similarly borrowed a day from the praetor, the plebeian aediles from the tribunes.

Voting was open in *iudicia populi* until 137, when Cassius

Longinus, tribune of the plebs, passed a plebiscite introducing the ballot for all trials except those for *perduellio*.[77] The ballot was extended to *perduellio* in 106 by C. Caelius, tribune of the plebs, to facilitate his prosecution of Popillius Laenas.[78]

The normal rules of veto applied to *iudicia populi*. We hear only of tribunes vetoing (or being asked or threatening to veto) each other or aediles,[79] unless Cicero as consul used his veto to stop the duumviral trial of Rabirius.[80] A trial might thus be prevented *ab initio* or stopped later in the proceedings, or a particular move, like a change of penalty, barred. It was unusual to prosecute a magistrate in office or *absens rei publicae causa* without his own consent, but this was not strict law, and the rule was maintained by the use or threat of the veto.[81] What is remarkable is how rarely the veto was used, or even sought or threatened, for arbitrary personal grounds. Postumius the *publicanus* hoped that his relative, the tribune Servilius Casca, would veto his trial, but Casca, from fear of the people and from shame, failed to do so.[82] Ti. Gracchus is said to have vetoed the execution of the sentence passed on L. Scipio merely on the ground of his distinguished achievements,[83] and on the same ground to have blocked the completion of P. Scipio's trial.[84] It would almost seem that there was a convention of the constitution whereby tribunes used their veto only to prevent breaches of customary rules of procedure such as the prosecution of a magistrate in office or the trial of the same defendant on the same charge twice.[85]

The prosecuting magistrate could drop a trial at any stage. The tribunes prosecuting Acilius Glabrio in 189 abandoned the case at the third *contio*, the tribune prosecuting the censor Gracchus in 169 the day before the final *comitia*.[86] If the actual *comitia* were vitiated by a rainstorm or similar evil omen the accused was deemed acquitted and could not be tried again. The most famous case is that of Claudius Pulcher in 248, and the later rule may be based on that precedent. Two tribunes first tried him for *perduellio* before the *comitia centuriata*, but the voting was stopped by a storm; when they tried again their colleagues vetoed them, 'ne idem homines in eodem magistratu perduellionis bis eundem accusarent'. They proceeded, however, to prosecute him successfully for a fine.[87]

The accused was very rarely arrested or even required to give bail. We know in fact of only one historical case: the tribunes on prosecuting the *publicanus* Postumius for riotously breaking up the *concilium plebis* at his previous trial demanded bail and threatened to imprison him if he refused to give it. They actually did imprison some of his supporters, either because they refused to give bail or, later, even if they offered it.[88] Normally the accused was merely cited for each hearing. In the case of T. Quinctius Rocus, accused on a capital charge, the trumpeter was instructed to blow the trumpet outside his door and tell him to present himself in the Campus Martius at dawn: this was for the final session of the trial.[89] The accused could plead illness as an excuse for not attending when summoned: P. Scipio in Valerius Antias' version of his final trial did so when summoned from Liternum to the third *contio*. The tribunes in this case refused to accept the excuse and postpone the hearing, but what would have happened next is not clear, as another tribune declared that he would not allow Scipio to be accused until he returned to Rome, and would, if appealed to, veto the trial.[90] When Postumius failed to appear without excuse, having been summoned on a capital charge, the tribunes moved and the plebs voted that 'if M. Postumius does not come forward before 1 May and being cited on that day does not respond and is not excused, he is deemed to be in exile and his goods are to be sold and he himself denied fire and water'.[91] According to Polybius the accused on a capital charge was customarily allowed to go into exile at any moment before the majority of tribes (he should have said 'centuries') had condemned him, and nearly all seem to have availed themselves of this privilege. The final step in the process was a plebiscite forbidding fire and water.[92] According to one version Q. Caepio was actually executed in prison, but this is apparently untrue; according to another he was imprisoned but released by a friendly tribune and went into exile.[93] There is no record of a heavy fine being thus evaded by voluntary exile except the highly suspect case of Camillus.[94] The procedure was that the successful prosecutor demanded sureties for the fine, and if they were refused he could imprison the condemned man, unless (as in one version of L. Scipio's case) a tribune vetoed.[95] This was the treatment accorded to persons of consequence found guilty of political offences. The humble offender does not seem to have been so leniently treated. We know of several cases where the *tresviri capitales* arrested people before trial and kept them in prison: the poet Naevius for his libellous verses, a centurion named Cornelius for sodomy, a certain P. Munatius for sacrilege.[96] Nor did humble people escape after trial: we are told of a freeborn woman, condemned on a capital charge, being kept in prison pending execution.[97]

In Cicero's ideal constitution all the magistrates had the right of *iudicium* (with appeal following),[98] but in fact the only magistrates recorded to have prosecuted were the tribunes of the plebs, the aediles, curule and plebeian, the quaestors and the *pontifex maximus*. To these must be added the specially appointed *duoviri perduellionis*, who dealt only with *perduellio*.[99] The *pontifex maximus* dealt only with (potential) neglect of their religious duties by the *rex* or the *flamines*.[100] The quaestors are recorded to have prosecuted on two occasions, once for murder and once on an unknown charge.[101] The tribunes in all recorded cases in the historical period dealt with what may be broadly called political cases. The aediles prosecuted on a great variety of charges. Some may be classified as political. The two plebeian aediles of 246 arraigned Claudia for remarking that she wished her brother would lose another big naval battle to make the streets of Rome less crowded.[102] The curule aedile A. Hostilius Mancinus (probably the *legatus* of 149) tried to prosecute a prostitute before the people for throwing a tile at him and wounding him. It is to be presumed that he did so because he claimed that the assault was an attack on his magisterial office, though in fact it took place in a drunken brawl which he had initiated.[103] Cicero threatened to bring charges of judicial corruption and provincial extortion as curule aedile[104]—charges which came under the *lex repetundarum*. Clodius as curule aedile prosecuted Milo *de vi* and threatened to prosecute Cicero, presumably for executing citizens without appeal.[105] Other charges, however, are for ordinary crimes. About 226 M. Claudius Marcellus curule, aedile, prosecuted C. Scantinius Capitolinus, (who was either aedile or tribune of the plebs) for *stuprum* (sodomy).[106] Metellus Celer was probably aedile (though perhaps tribune) when he prosecuted a man for attempted *stuprum* (adultery) in the first half of the first century.[107] Spurius Albinus, curule aedile, prosecuted a freedman, C. Furius Chresimus, for charming his neighbours' crops on to his own land by magic. The very circumstantial story is told by Piso (who was consul in 133), and the Greek freedman suggests a second-century date: the only known Sp. Albinus of this period was praetor in 189 and could have been aedile in 191.[108] In 192 the two curule aediles, M. Tuccius and P. Junius Brutus, prosecuted a large number of moneylenders, presumably for exceeding the legal rate of interest, and erected a monument from the fines; and in 189 the two curule and one of the plebeian aediles condemned a number of corn merchants for making a corner in wheat.[109]

The political charges brought by tribunes (and occasionally aediles) are singularly hard to define. The brief allusions and even the longer accounts which we have often fail to distinguish between the actual charge or charges, the alleged motive of the prosecutor—often a personal grievance against the accused or a long-standing enmity with him—and the general raking up of all the misdeeds, public or private, of the accused which was the general habit of prosecutors. It is only rarely, as in the prosecution of the censors of 169, that the first two can be sorted out. The moving force behind that prosecution was the anger of the *publicani* at being excluded by the censors from bidding for public contracts. A tribune, P. Rutilius, was induced to make an attack on the censors because a freedman of his had been ordered to demolish a building which he had erected on public land, and fined by the censors despite his having appealed to the tribune. Rutilius proposed a bill annulling the allocation of contracts and ordering a new auction, and at a *contio* one of the censors, on being howled down, ordered the *praeco* to quell the tumult. The tribune now initiated a prosecution of both censors on the charge that they had infringed his sacrosanctity, Gracchus by enforcing a fine contrary to his veto and Claudius by calling the *contio* away from him. The formal charge was thus *perduellio*.[110]

In these circumstances it is often difficult to define the precise charge or charges. In the much discussed final trial of Scipio Africanus, in one version a tribune accuses him of having taken a bribe from Antiochus III to give him a favourable treaty of peace, and of other things. In the other main version, that of Valerius Antias, the tribunes began by referring to discreditable incidents earlier in Scipio's career, to alleged luxury when at Syracuse and to the Pleminius affair; but these were not brought as charges but as evidence of character. The charges were vague allegations or suspicions of *pecunia capta*, the fact that his son was returned to him by Antiochus without reason, and that he was flattered by Antiochus. The tribunes ended with a general denunciation of his dictatorial conduct as his brother's legate. Here it would seem that the intention of the prosecutors was to suggest that Scipio had been bribed or unduly influenced to give Antiochus a favourable treaty, but if this charge was specifically made it could not be proved, and no doubt provable facts like the return of Scipio's son and friendly interviews and correspondence with Antiochus were put on the charge sheet: according to Polybius there were many charges.[111]

The types of charge that can be distinguished include: neglect of the auspices (Claudius Pulcher before the disastrous defeat of the Roman fleet at Drepanum in 249);[112] making war—with disastrous results—without the authorization of the senate or people (Aemilius Lepidus in 137 and Junius Silanus in 104);[113] cowardice in command of an army (Fulvius Flaccus in 211);[114] capitulation of an army (C. Popilius Laenas in 106).[115] With these cases may be associated those of other unsuccessful generals where the precise charge is unknown: Sulpicius Galba in 149 (perhaps his treacherous attack on the surrendered Lusitanians); C. Plautius, also in Spain, in 146; and Mallius and Caepio in 103 (perhaps failure to co-operate against the Cimbri).[116] Then there are charges of *peculatus* of booty or war indemnities (Livius and Aemilius Paulus, the consuls of 219, Acilius Glabrio in 189, P. Scipio in 187 and L. Scipio in 184),[117] and of oppression of allied communities in time of war (Pleminius, *legatus* at Locri in 205–4; Lucretius in various Aegean cities in 171).[118] A magistrate might be prosecuted for neglect of his religious duties (Aemilius Scaurus in 104)[119] or his official functions (the *tresviri capitales* on two occasions).[120] The censors were frequently prosecuted or threatened with prosecution, it would seem for abuse of their powers, but precise details are lacking (Atilius and Furius in 213; Livius and Claudius in 204; Cato in 184; Scipio Aemilianus in 140).[121] Claudius and Sempronius Gracchus in 169 were officially tried for violating the *tribunicia sacrosanctitas*, as was Postumius the *publicanus* at his second trial in 212; in his first trial the accusation was cheating the treasury.[122] Popilius Laenas and Rupilius, the consuls of 132, and Opimius, the consul of 121, were tried for executing Roman citizens without appeal, as was Rabirius in 63.[123] Metellus was prosecuted in 100 for refusing to take an oath prescribed by law, the tribune Furius apparently for vetoing

Metellus' recall.[124] Nearly all the accused were magistrates or promagistrates or at least legates or senators. The very few private persons accused include Claudia, Postumius, Rabirius, the prostitute who threw a brick at an aedile, a citizen accused in 43 of supporting a *regnum* at Rome,[125] and—in a rather melodramatic story from Diodorus—the widow and sons of Regulus (cos. 256) for gross cruelty to prominent Carthaginian prisoners entrusted to their care.[126]

Some of these cases were based on specific statutes, such as the various *leges de provocatione*, reaffirmed by C. Gracchus' law of 123, or the *lex agraria* of Saturninus under which Metellus was prosecuted. Some may have been brought under a law on *peculatus*: no early statute is known, and it may have depended on the Twelve Tables. Most may be classed under *perduellio*, which received some definition in the Twelve Tables.[127] But it would be misleading to try to bring all the charges under some specific legal category. Any act of a magistrate which was contrary to *mores maiorum* might be made the basis of an accusation. The tribunes could judge *vel legibus vel moribus*. The tribune Sempronius Blaesus began by prosecuting Gnaeus Fulvius for a fine for joining in the rout of his army—'conduct unbecoming an officer and a gentleman'. When he discovered that Fulvius had initiated the flight the offence came within the bounds of *perduellio* and he wished to make the charge capital. The other tribunes, when an appeal was made to them, replied that they had no objection to Sempronius, according to ancient custom, conducting the trial either by custom or by law, so long as he gave judgment on the prisoner either capitally or for a fine. The second part of the proceedings was clearly *legibus*, for *perduellio*, the first part *moribus*.[128] The concept *moribus* was evidently elastic: the tribune Furius had broken no law by vetoing a bill; his only offence, *moribus*, was to have baulked the popular desire to restore the hero Metellus. And Claudia was prosecuted simply for insulting the Roman people.

Iudicia populi were clearly provided for in the constitution laid down for the Lucanian city of Bantia, a constitution closely modelled on that of Rome, and dating from some time in the second century B.C.[129] In one clause the magistrate holding *comitia* 'for *x* or money' must cause the people to swear that they will deliver sentence for the best in the public interest; and in the next the magistrate who declares a day against anyone 'for *x* or money' must not hold the *comitia* until he has pleaded ('oraverit', trans.) four times before the people on announced days, after which he is to fix a day at least thirty days in advance for judgment.[130] Except that there are four preliminary *contiones*, the Roman model is followed exactly.

Iudicia populi for political offences are far more commonly reported in the surviving historical tradition than *iudicia populi* for ordinary crimes, but this is only natural seeing that historians were primarily concerned with political affairs. A sufficient number of *iudicia populi* for the crimes of the common man survive in our record to make credible Cicero's view that all crimes were dealt with by this process. There is moreover no evidence of any other form of trial, except when on rare occasions the people or the senate set up special commissions to deal with particular cases, as will be described later. The main objection—apart from alleged lack of evidence—to the view that the *iudicium populi* was the normal procedure for trying crimes, whether the penalty was death or a fine above a certain minimum, is that crime cannot have been efficiently repressed in a large city like Rome (or for that matter over the vast extent of the *ager Romanus*) by so cumbrous a procedure. In the first place there is no reason to believe that crime *was* efficiently repressed: the fact that in the second century the senate occasionally ordered special *quaestiones* for murder, poisoning or other capital crimes in Rome and Roman territory rather suggests that at times public opinion became alarmed at the prevalence of crime. The system had been satisfactory for a small town such as Rome once was—and the Roman commissioner or the people of Bantia thought it all right for *that* small town. If in a huge city it no longer worked it may have been tolerated by inertia; after all the British government in similar circumstances for generations tolerated a judicial system which failed to suppress widespread violent crime in London.

It must be remembered moreover that the two commonest offences today regarded as crimes, theft and assault, were handled by the civil courts. The *iudicia populi*, so far as we know, dealt only with murder, *stuprum* (adultery and sodomy), some forms of maleficent magic, perhaps arson (though there is no evidence), exceeding the maximum rate of interest or the maximum holding of public land, and making a corner in wheat. It has also often been noted that *provocatio* (and trial before the people) did not apply to slaves and foreigners, who came to form a considerable portion of the population of Rome. It did, of course, come to apply to Roman citizens everywhere.

In strict law, it is generally agreed, *provocatio* was originally valid only within the *pomerium* or up to one mile beyond it.[131] Theoretically, then, a magistrate might condemn without appeal, even inflicting the death penalty, anywhere in Roman territory, and no doubt on Roman citizens in allied communities in Italy and the provinces. Actually, condemnations were unlikely to occur in Italy, as all Roman magistrates were usually occupied in Rome or in the provinces. It appears, however, that in the third century there was a strong feeling against the execution (even after trial) of Roman citizens outside Rome. The best documented case is that of Q. Pleminius, who was put in command of the garrison at Locri as *legatus* by Scipio in 205 and encouraged his troops to maltreat the Locrians and rob the local temple of Proserpina. When two military tribunes resisted him he ordered them to be flogged, and a general mutiny followed. Scipio returned to Locri, acquitted Pleminius and adjudged the two tribunes guilty, but did not execute them but sent them in chains to the senate at Rome. The Locrians sent a delegation to the senate. Senators hostile to Scipio took advantage of the situation to suggest that, if responsible, he should be recalled from Sicily. It was also proposed that Pleminius should be sent in chains to Rome, to plead his case in chains, and if the charges were proved be executed in prison and his goods confiscated; it is not stated how the case was to be tried or by whom. Eventually the senate sent M. Pomponius, the praetor to whom Sicily had been allotted, with ten legates and two tribunes of the plebs and an aedile, with instructions that the praetor, using the legates as his *consilium*, was to try the case at Locri. If he judged that Scipio was responsible the two tribunes and the aedile were to proceed to Africa and recall Scipio to Rome, using their sacrosanct power to seize him if he resisted. (The senate was apparently oblivious of the rule that a tribune's sacrosanctity ceased one mile from Rome.) When the party arrived at Locri the Locrians declared that Scipio had not been responsible, and the praetor gladly accepted their assurances. He condemned Pleminius and thirty-two others and sent them in chains to Rome. He had received no express instructions as to what to do with them, but he could legally have executed them on condemnation. Pleminius died in prison at Rome before a *iudicium populi* could be held. Nothing is said of the fate of the thirty-two others, who must have included persons of quite humble rank, at the most centurions, except that they were produced before the people by a tribune of the plebs, which suggests a *iudicium populi*.[132]

When Capua surrendered in 211 after its rebellion the two proconsuls on the spot, Claudius Pulcher and Fulvius Flaccus, disagreed about what they were to do with the fifty-three senators of Capua (who were Roman citizens *sine suffragio*) who had been arrested. Claudius wanted to refer their fate to the senate, but Fulvius was determined to execute them, and did so before the senate's reply to Claudius' despatch was received. He also executed about seventy other Campanian senators, those of Atella and Calatia. When the fate of the Campanians came to be debated in the senate Atilius Regulus declared: 'I do not see that any action can be taken about the Campanians, who are Roman citizens, by the senate without the order of the people', and therefore proposed that the tribunes of the plebs be asked to move a bill whereby the senate might be empowered to decide about the Campanians. The plebs duly enacted that 'we wish and command whatever the majority of the senate may decide upon oath'. The senate was not very severe, ordering some Campanian families to be sold into slavery and others to be imprisoned pending further investigation. Fulvius Flaccus contrived to make ruthless use of his *imperium*, executing 170 Campanians alleged to have plotted arson against the Roman camp.[133]

Shortly after 282 a Campanian legion which was garrisoning Rhegium emulated their kinsmen the Mamertines and seized the town for themselves. In 278 Fabricius (cos. II) reduced the town, arrested the ringleaders (perhaps 300 in number) and sent them in chains to Rome, where with the support of the senate the consuls flogged and executed them publicly. A tribune of the plebs, M. Fulvius Flaccus, protested at this execution of Roman citizens contrary to ancestral custom. Later there was a second rebellion of the Campanian legion at Rhegium, and the consul Genucius sent the whole body to Rome, where they were condemned by the people and executed.[134]

It is, then, in fact, very rarely that Roman citizens, even if rebels or mutinous soldiers, are executed by a Roman magistrate in Italy. They are normally sent to Rome and either tried by the people or by the senate with special authorisation from the people. No distinction seems to have been made between senators like Pleminius and common soldiers. Only once does a proconsul (Fulvius Flaccus) exercise his legal right to try and execute Roman citizens on the spot, and they are rebel Campanians. Further afield, where it was impracticable to send men to Rome, proconsuls no doubt used their legal powers more freely: Scipio condemned and publicly flogged and executed mutineers in Spain in 206.[135]

When and how the formal right of *provocatio* outside Rome was established it is very difficult to say. There were three Porcian laws on *provocatio*, which are commonly placed in the first half of the second century but cannot be precisely dated. They are said by Cicero to have imposed severer sanctions on magistrates who neglected *provocatio* but to have made no other change.[136] According to Livy 'the (or 'a') Porcian law alone seems to have been passed on behalf of the back (*tergo*) of citizens, because it provided a severe penal sanction if anyone flogged or executed a Roman citizen'.[137] This is a comment on the absence of a sanction from the *lex Valeria de provocatione* of 300, and its general drift supports Cicero, in spite of its irrelevant stress on *provocatio* against flogging. Caesar's speech in the Catilinarian debate of 63 B.C., as reported by Sallust, also links a *lex Porcia* with flogging. He argues: if you are proposing to execute the conspirators without appeal, why do you not propose to flog them first? 'Is it because the (or 'a') Porcian law forbids it? But then other laws order that condemned citizens shall not be put to death but allowed to go into exile.'[138]

The general tradition was that earlier laws (including the *lex Valeria* of 300, whose text seems to have been known) allowed appeal against flogging and execution. It may have been held that this meant the traditional penalty of flogging-plus-execution, and a *lex Porcia* may have made it clear that appeal covered also a sentence of flogging alone: Rabirius was charged with flogging *or* executing Roman citizens, apparently in Campania and Apulia (as *tribunus militum* in 89?) contrary to a *lex Porcia*.[139] It is likely that protests against Roman magistrates flogging and executing allies, particularly magistrates of allied towns in Italy, imply that Roman citizens were protected against such treatment; the earliest of such protests is a speech of Cato, probably delivered in 190.[140] Further, the well-known coin issued by, and alluding to the ancestry of, the moneyer P. Laeca, probably shortly before 100 B.C., has on its reverse the legend PROVOCO and the representation of a man in armour and *paludamentum*—presumably a Roman consul or praetor outside Rome—standing and putting his hand on the head of a man in a toga, and a third figure holding a rod in one hand and two in the other.[141] It is a reasonable interpretation that Laeca was honouring the memory of an ancestor who passed a law *de provocatione*, who may be the P. Porcius Laeca who was tribune of the plebs in 199 and praetor in 195. The scene clearly takes place before a magistrate outside the pomerium, and the third figure is a lictor preparing to flog (not execute) the appellant.

In 125 the consul M. Fulvius Flaccus proposed a law giving to the Italian allies either Roman citizenship or *provocatio ad populum* to those who preferred not to change their citizenship.[142] In 123–2 the *lex Acilia* similarly seems to have offered to successful prosecutors under that law who were Latins the choice of *civitas* or *provocatio*.[143] In 122 Livius Drusus, as a counterblast to C. Gracchus' law giving citizenship to the Latins, proposed a law that Latins should not be allowed to be flogged even on military service.[144] It is politically inconceivable that Latins or other allies can have been offered a greater privilege than Roman citizens possessed at the time, and perhaps unlikely that the right should be specified in a law unless that same right was guaranteed by a law to Romans. The right was, if Plutarch's description of the bill of Livius is correct, of *provocatio* against flogging (and *a fortiori* the death penalty) even on military service (and *a fortiori* for civilians anywhere). For Latins and allies, incidentally, *provocatio* would be of little use in practice if it were not available on military service (where alone they normally came under Roman magistrates) and in their own towns (against such arbitrary floggings by travelling Roman magistrates as Cato and C. Gracchus describe).[145]

A test case would be provided—if Sallust's style were not so perverse and the other authorities so careless—by the execution for military misconduct in 109, by Metellus the proconsul in Africa, of T. Turpilius Silanus, prefect of the garrison at Vaga.

Turpilius is described by Appian as a Roman and by Plutarch as *praefectus fabrum*. Sallust says that Metellus ordered him to make his defence, and as it was unsatisfactory he was condemned, flogged and executed, 'nam is civis e Latio erat'.[146] It has been argued that Turpilius was a Roman citizen from a Latin town (e.g. an ex-magistrate of the town). This entails the preposterous view that if he had been a Latin he could not have been executed, but could be because he was a Roman. Further, on this view, why did Sallust feel the need to account for Turpilius being executed, except on the unlikely hypothesis that his readers would think Turpilius was a Latin? (It is very unlikely that they would know anything about so obscure a character, and from his name and post the natural assumption would be that he was a Roman.) The most sensible view is that Sallust thought it necessary to give an explanation for the execution of an apparently Roman officer, viz. that he was actually a Latin.

There is another curious fact to remark. As we have seen, a Roman commander in Spain in 206 executed mutineers *more maiorum* with flogging and the axe. Polybius, who first became acquainted with a Roman army operating in the provinces in the middle of the second century--to be precise, probably first in 151 in Spain and certainly in Africa and Achaea in the next five years —describes a quite different procedure. After an offender has been judged and condemned at the council of tribunes (it is to be presumed that the commander presided and actually gave judgment) the tribune takes a stick and just touches the condemned soldier, who then has to run the gauntlet of the assembled army and rarely escapes alive. The same procedure was used for decimation after the victims had been chosen by lot.[147] Why did Roman commanders give up orderly official execution for this organised lynching? The simplest answer is that they did not want to make themselves liable to a *lex de provocatione* by officially executing a soldier. And it seems more likely that they feared a specific legal prohibition than *mos maiorum*; in distant provinces it was *mos maiorum* at the end of the third century to execute soldiers, though it was not in Italy in the 280's. There was apparently a similar evasion of the law about scourging: Scipio outside Numantia in a rigorous restoration of discipline had allies flogged *virgis* but Romans with the centurion's cane (*vitibus*).[148]

It may be inferred that *provocatio* was legally extended outside Rome to cover Italy and the provinces and soldiers as well as civilians, probably (*pace* Cicero) by a *lex Porcia*, and that it was extended to protect from mere scourging. This change had happened well before 150 (Polybius regarded *fustigatio-fustuarium* as established practice) and perhaps as early as 190, when Cato protested against the flogging of Italian civilians in Italy. But the territorial extension of *provocatio* may not have been due to the same *lex Porcia* as its extension to flogging, and it may have been at different dates that civilians and soldiers outside Rome acquired it.

To return to the argument about the weakness or inefficiency of *iudicia populi*, the main weaknesses of the Roman criminal system applied as much to the era of the *iudicia publica* as to that of the *iudicia populi*. There was no police force, and the detection of criminals was normally left to injured parties or common informers. Criminal justice was, moreover, in both eras fantastically centralized, with no court except at Rome—though it must be admitted that there were several at Rome in the later period, by which time they had to cover the whole of Italy south of the Po. It may also be questioned whether the system of *iudicia populi* was more cumbersome or time-wasting than that of the *iudicia publica*. Under the latter a given trial might occupy a magistrate and about fifty senators or *equites* for several weeks: a *iudicium populi* occupied four days at the maximum for a magistrate, and might take much less— a *contio* might last half an hour and a meeting of the *comitia* not much longer. And there was no quorum for *contiones* or *comitia*, still less any quorum of senators or *equites*.

There are indications that the three *contiones* might in some circumstances be omitted. The clearest is Cicero's remark that if Clodius as aedile in 56 had initiated a prosecution of him he (Cicero) would have arranged that the praetor should fix the day (for the *comitia* which voted) on the day after tomorrow.[149] With the accused's consent, then, there need be only one session, and that immediately. The censors of 169 seem to have agreed to this shortened procedure: 'the censors did not object against the people's passing judgment on them as soon as possible, and the day was fixed (by the praetor) for the *comitia* for *perduellio* on 24 and 25 Oct.'. The narrative proceeds at once to a meeting at which Claudius pleads his case and the vote is taken.[150] In one case the shortened procedure appears to have been used when the accused is not said to have assented and is unlikely to have done so. The whole trial of Postumius the *publicanus*, including evidence, is represented as taking place on the same day as the vote (which Postumius and his backers stopped by violence). This may be dramatic compression, but it is possible that the three *contiones* were only prescribed *more maiorum* (unlike execution without a vote of the people, which was contrary to statute), and that if no tribune objected a magistrate could fairly safely omit them; in Postumius' case popular feeling was very hostile to him, and only one tribune was his friend, and that a timorous man. It is even possible that a magistrate might go further still and dispense with the popular vote altogether, if, for instance, the accused confessed (under the kind of bullying of which magistrates were quite capable) or was caught red-handed, and no tribune would object. There is, however, no evidence of such summary justice: on the contrary even common soldiers whose offences had been proved before a magistrate in the field were put before the people—or violent protests were made if they were not. The only difference between the lot of upper and lower class offenders seems to have been that the latter were frequently, perhaps regularly, imprisoned before trial and actually executed after it.

Efficient or otherwise, the conclusion remains that the *iudicia populi* were the only regular organ of criminal justice. A capital jurisdiction has recently been assigned to the *tresviri capitales*.[151] They were first instituted about 290 B.C. and at some later date (after 241 B.C.) made elective by a *lex Papiria*,[152] having presumably been down to that time nominated by the praetor. One of their functions was to patrol the city at night—whence their unofficial title of *tresviri nocturni*—to prevent fires and apprehend nocturnal criminals.[153] They also received information laid against malefactors and took into custody offenders brought to them at the Columna Maenia.[154] They maintained the prison, guarded suspects before trial and executed the condemned.[155] The *lex Papiria* directed that the *tresviri* 'sacramenta exigunto iudicantoque, eodemque iure sunto uti ex legibus plebeique scitis exigere iudicareque esseque oportet':[156] the phrase 'to exact and judge *sacramenta*' is obscure, but can hardly mean to try cases by *legis actio sacramento*, for such very junior magistrates could not have had concurrent jurisdiction with the praetor. It probably means to exact from defeated civil litigants the *sacramenta* that were consequently payable to the praetor, with such judicial power as was required for the purpose. The *tresviri* may have acquired some wider judicial powers: Q. Aelius Tubero may have held that post when he decided that an augur was not exempt from the duty of serving as a judge, and the phrase 'trium virorum capitalium iudicium' is discussed in the *Orator*.[157] But there is no convincing evidence that they exercised a criminal—let alone a capital—jurisdiction.

Now between the years 186 and 179 the senate appears to have become conscious of a problem of crime in Rome and Italy. It all started with the discovery in 186 that there was a widespread secret Bacchanalian cult which was supposed to encourage immorality. We have a very full account of the whole affair in Livy as well as a contemporary copy of the *senatus consultum*. The senate declared the Bacchanalian cult to be a capital offence and instructed both consuls to hold an investigation *extra ordinem*. The consuls ordered the aediles to round up all Bacchanalian priests and the *tresviri capitales* to establish patrols to prevent meetings. Rewards were offered to informers. The investigation was pursued not only in Rome but in the country towns of the Roman territory and in allied cities. Though no figures are given, the impression is conveyed that large numbers of citizens were executed.[158]

In 184 Naevius Matho, the praetor to whom Sardinia was allotted, was instructed to investigate cases of poisoning, mostly outside the city in the country towns, and spent four months on the task before proceeding to his province. According to Valerius Antias he condemned 2,000 persons. In the same year Postumius, the praetor allocated to Tarentum, carried on trials of Bacchanalians, mostly refugees from Rome; some he condemned, others he sent to Rome. Next year Pupius, praetor of Apulia, carried on the task until he was relieved by Duronius, the praetor allotted to Apulia in 181. In 180 the senate instructed Claudius the peregrine praetor to investigate poisoning in Rome and within ten miles, and Maenius, who was allocated Sardinia, to do the same in Roman territory outside the ten-mile limit. He later reported that he had condemned 3,000 persons and would never get to his province if he went on with the trials. The trials in Rome were continued next year by Mucius Scaevola the urban praetor.[159] The senate then took no action for over twelve years: this is a fairly safe assumption, as we have the full narrative of Livy, who notes each year the tasks of each praetor. In 167 Manlius Torquatus, allocated Sardinia, was directed by the senate to investigate capital cases and never got to Sardinia.[160] A year after this Livy's narrative comes to an end. There may well have been other special *quaestiones* later: Polybius regarded the suppression of conspiracies, murder and poisoning in Italy as a function of the senate.[161] We are told that Hostilius Tubulus, praetor in 142, made himself notorious for corruption as judge in murder trials.[162]

This series of special *quaestiones* clearly demonstrates that it was not, as some allege, the normal duty of the praetors to judge criminal cases. Why should the senate have to pass a resolution instructing the urban or peregrine praetor to undertake this or that piece of criminal jurisdiction if it was part of their normal duties? And surely it was not normal for a provincial praetor to delay his arrival in his province for several months, or not set foot in it at all?

There were also investigations ordered by the senate for *causes célèbres*. The case of Pleminius and his associates has already been described.[163] In 187 L. Scipio, his two legates, his *scribae* and *accensus* were tried for peculation (this is according to a probably bogus version of the affair by Valerius Antias, but may serve to illustrate procedure).[164] The process was started by a plebiscite ordering the urban praetor to ask the senate to appoint a praetor to investigate peculations concerned with King Antiochus. The senate appointed Terentius Culleo, and on information received the persons mentioned were tried, and some acquitted and some condemned. In 172 two tribunes, with the approval of the senate, moved a plebiscite empowering the senate to appoint a judge to investigate the unlawful injuries inflicted on the Ligures Statiellates and punish their author, Popillius Laenas the consul of the previous year. The senate appointed one of the praetors, who examined Laenas but allowed the case to lapse.[165] In the case of the corrupt praetor of 142, Tubulus, mentioned above, a tribune moved a plebiscite ordering an enquiry into his conduct, under which the senate appointed one of the consuls to try him.[166]

In 138 some important people were murdered in the Sila, it was suspected by free employees of the company which worked the local forest for pitch. The senate appointed the consuls to try the suspects. This is one of the few cases where we have some details of the proceedings. The company employed eminent counsel, there were more than three sessions of the court, and the consuls acted *de consilii sententia* like all Roman magistrates, that is to say with assessors of their own choice to advise them.[167] In 132 the senate instructed the consuls to try the adherents of Tiberius Gracchus, and they condemned large numbers to death; here again we happen to know that they acted with a *consilium*.[168] In 121 again Opimius, one of the consuls, presumably on the senate's advice, tried adherents of C. Gracchus; he is said to have condemned over 3,000 persons to death.[169]

In none of these trials is there a hint of appeal. The refusal of *provocatio* would have been legal if the people had by law or plebiscite vested the senate or judges with their powers, as was done with the Campanians in 211, with L. Scipio and his staff in 187 (according to Antias) and with Tubulus in 141. But in no other case is there reference to a law or plebiscite, although for the Bacchanalian affair the narrative is very circumstantial and throughout we have a tolerably full record from Livy. It looks as if in these as in many matters the senate unconcernedly usurped what was legally a right of the people—just as the senate regularly decreed *prorogatio* of *imperium*, which, as the very word used shows, was properly a matter for a law of the people. Protest was only raised when the courts decreed by the senate in 132 and 121 had a strong political bias.

Now that the workings of the *iudicia populi* have been examined during the historical period it remains to see what can be said about earlier stages and, ultimately, about origins. The memory of Fabius Pictor, the first Roman historian, and his older contemporaries would not have extended before the middle of the third century B.C. For earlier events he and later historians had to rely on tradition, usually unreliable beyond, say, a century, and on what official written records there were. The *annales* of the *pontifices* seem to have been fairly full (and the entries, being contemporary, reliable) for some time back; but we do not know how far back there were genuine and full *annales*. There were also books of the *pontifices* and augurs which contained old precedents; again we cannot tell how far back genuine precedents went. There existed also, important for the subject of this book, the full text of the Twelve Tables, which even radically-minded scholars admit were probably enacted in the middle of the fifth century; the language seems to have been somewhat modernised in transmission, but the few verbal quotations surviving are pretty archaic in language and content.

In a process of working backwards from the historical period towards the time of the Twelve Tables there is first the trial of L. Postumius, consul in 291, by two tribunes. It looks like a normal 'political' trial, the charges being given as: employing troops to cultivate his private estates, distributing all the booty to his men and discharging them before his successor arrived, and celebrating an unauthorised triumph. He had been prosecuted by a tribune in 293 for an unstated offence, but had escaped trial by going off as the consul's legate.[170] Then there are two tribunician trials for sodomy, rather vaguely dated to the last quarter of the fourth century. Both have political overtones—a military tribune using his authority to seduce a soldier and a creditor trying to bend his debtor bondman to his will by beating him up.[171] The circumstances may account for tribunes of the plebs conducting trials for ordinary crime. There are quite routine trials by aediles in 296 for usury and grazing too many cattle on public land, in 298 and 293 for occupying too much public land:[172] such dull information can only have come from records. In 295 Q. Fabius Gurges prosecuted before the people a number of married women on charges of adultery; he is presumed, from the offence, to have been aedile, and the information may come from an inscription on a temple which he built from the fines.[173] In 329 Flavius Augur was prosecuted by the aedile C. Valerius before the tribal assembly for adultery. We are told that when fourteen tribes had condemned him Flavius cried out that he was innocent, and Valerius said he did not mind if he was innocent as long as he was condemned, and the other tribes all voted for acquittal, and he was acquitted. The anecdote is at least accurate in implying that there were 29 tribes, which there were between 332 and 318.[174] More routine trials by aediles for usury are recorded in 345,[175] which makes it credible (even if the story is too good to be true) that Licinius Stolo, the author of the law limiting occupation of public land, was convicted in 357 for that very offence by Popilius

Laenas, presumably an aedile.[176] The tribunician political trial in 362 of L. Manlius, an ex-dictator, for exceeding his six months of office and (perhaps 'or') severity in the military call-up is chiefly celebrated because the prosecuting tribune made great play with the fact that Manlius kept his son in durance on a country farm, and the son, hearing of this, threatened to kill the tribune if he persisted in the prosecution.[177]

Next in reverse order comes the trial of Manlius Capitolinus in 384, highly overlaid by romance. There were two versions: that he was prosecuted by two tribunes or by *duoviri perduellionis*. It was anyhow before the *comitia centuriata*.[178] In 389 the tribune Cn. Marcius prosecuted Q. Fabius for violating international law by fighting the Gauls when he was an envoy to them.[179] In 391 Camillus is said to have been tried by a tribune or else by a quaestor (presumably one of the ordinary pair), before the *comitia centuriata* according to Cicero, according to other authorities for a fine of various amounts—which implies the tribal assembly. The best-attested charge is maldistribution or misappropriation of spoils.[180] Next is the trial of two tribunes of the plebs by the tribunes of the next year, 393, for using their veto to defeat the will of the plebs.[181] In 401, 420 and 424 are trials for military misconduct of sundry consuls and *tribuni militum consulari potestate*:[182] the persons involved are obscure and the charges of no interest, and it is difficult to see why they should have been invented or falsified. Of greater interest to later generations, and therefore more suspect, is the prosecution by Sp. Maelius, tribune of the plebs in 436, of Servilius Ahala, who had killed—as a private citizen or as *magister equitum*—the prosecutor's more famous kinsman Sp. Maelius, who was alleged to have aspired to *regnum*. The tribune is also said to have prosecuted one Minucius for false witness against his kinsman. Cicero says that Ahala was tried before the *comitia centuriata*; Livy mentions only a plebiscite to confiscate his goods, which might be consequential on his going into exile to avoid condemnation.[183] Only one more item lies between this case and the date of the Twelve Tables: the tribunician prosecutions of Appius Claudius and other *decemviri*. They are highly dramatised and not very interesting.[184]

In this period also there are some special commissions authorised by the people or the senate in special cases. In 314 there was a rebellion at Capua, a town of Roman citizens, and the senate got a dictator appointed. He recaptured the town and was commissioned to investigate the conspiracy there—either that which had led to the rebellion or one that occurred after it. Capital trials were involved. He could as dictator at that date presumably execute citizens without appeal, and he did so. He also interpreted his commission as including all conspiracies, and transferred his activities to Rome, where he tried persons alleged to have conspired to achieve election to offices. Those accused appealed to the tribunes in vain. Eventually the dictator and his *magister equitum* resigned and submitted to the judgment of the consuls (the senate delegating the investigation to them) on the very same charge of electoral conspiracy; they were acquitted.[185] In this last phase the senate seems to be exceeding its legal powers. When the punishment of the Campanians was debated in 210 the precedent of Satricum was quoted: on that occasion, it was alleged in the senate, M. Antistius, tribune of the plebs, at the request of the senate had moved a plebiscite that the senate should have the right of passing sentence on the Satricans, like the Campanians a community of Roman citizens who had rebelled and were reduced in 319.[186] The evidence here seems fairly sound, and there is therefore little reason to doubt that when in 414 there was a mutiny in which a military tribune with consular power and his quaestor were killed and the senate proposed to deal with the mutineers, the tribunes of the plebs vetoed their action and ultimately, on the request of the senate, moved a plebiscite that the plebs should choose judges—and they chose the consuls of 413, who executed a few of the mutineers.[187]

It was in 300 that one of the consuls passed a *Lex Valeria de provocatione*, traditionally the third of that title. It is said to have forbidden that any citizen be flogged and killed with the axe by a magistrate without appeal, and to have had a 'more careful sanction', viz. that if anyone infringed it the deed was 'improbe factum'.[188] Later Roman lawyers and historians were puzzled what this meant: modern critics have almost unanimously declared that there could not have been three *leges Valeriae de provocatione* and that this was the only and the first law (they have not similarly argued that there was only onc *lex Porcia de provocatione* instead of the reputed three. And it is to be observed that in the tradition capital trials before the people, which in later times at any rate arose by *provocatio*, do not begin from 300).

There are several possible explanations for the repetition of a law on the same subject. The content may not have been identical: actually the second *lex Valeria* in 449 is said to have enacted that no magistracy should in future be created *sine provocatione* like the *decemviri*,[189] and the third in 300 is said to have been 'diligentius sancta'. The Porcian laws are also said to have laid down heavier penalties, and apparently extended the range of appeal, as was argued earlier in this chapter.[190] It is also possible, as Livy says about the third *lex Valeria*, that 'the reason for the renewal of the law was, I think, that the resources of the rich were more powerful than the liberty of the plebs',[191] in other words that in cases of poor citizens the law was often flouted. The main reason for the *lex Sempronia* of 123[192] was simply to reassert *provocatio* against the gradual usurpation of criminal jurisdiction without appeal by magistrates acting under *senatus consulta*; and finally either Julius Caesar or Augustus had to reaffirm *provocatio* by the *lex Iulia de vi publica*.[193] Two citations from the Twelve Tables are relevant to the issue. Cicero several times quotes a law which forbade 'de capite civis rogari nisi maximo comitiatu' (with unimportant verbal variations. Cicero understood *maximus comitiatus* to mean the *comitia centuriata*).[194] This surely implies capital trials before the assembly as already a normal procedure; *privilegia*, laws affecting a named person only, were by another frequently cited law of the Twelve Tables forbidden altogether.[195] Secondly, Cicero says that 'in several laws the Twelve Tables make it plain that it is legal to appeal from every judgment and penalty'.[196] It is ridiculous to suppose that Cicero did not know his Twelve Tables. If *provocatio* from any judgment or penalty already existed in the Twelve Tables it seems hypercritical to deny an earlier law which provided for *provocatio*. There is nothing incredible in a *lex Valeria* of 509; Solon had granted appeal from all judgments of magistrates to the people eighty years earlier, and even in the backward kingdom of Macedon in cases of treason an appeal could by ancient custom be made from the king to the people.[197]

Iudicia populi between 509 and 451 are likely to be even more mythical than those of a later period. They are in fact, as reported, just like later trials: Coriolanus for attacking the rights of the plebs and in particular the sacrosanctity of their tribunes in 491 (allegedly the first tribunician trial);[198] various consuls or ex-consuls by pairs of tribunes for alleged military misconduct in 476, 475, 473, 470, 454 (in the last of these years the accusers are exceptionally a tribune in one case and an aedile in the other);[199] a private citizen, Kaeso Quinctius, for insulting the tribunes in 461—the original test case for giving bail for appearance.[200] There is a trial by the quaestors of a private citizen for false witness in 458;[201] and finally the highly dramatised trial of Sp. Cassius, consul in 486, for attempting or plotting *regnum* (which was *perduellio*). Apart from a story in Valerius Maximus that he was tribune of the plebs and condemned by his father in a domestic court—contradicted by Valerius Maximus himself in another passage—Cassius is agreed to have been prosecuted or condemned in a *iudicium populi* by the quaestors: Livy names the two, Kaeso Fabius and L. Valerius, while Cicero merely says a quaestor accused (as usual, the one of the pair who actually gave judgment).[202]

Three problems of origins remain to be discussed: the role of the quaestors and *duoviri perduellionis*; the origin and nature of the criminal jurisdiction of the tribunes and aediles; and the origin of appeal against the higher fines. The two quaestors were originally assistants of the Kings and the consuls, and, according to Tacitus, nominated by them until 447, after which they were elected by the people.[203] Ulpian cites authorities who dated the quaestors back to Romulus; he is certain that they existed under Tullus Hostilius and says that the 'majority of ancient opinion' was that Tullus invented them (which might be a reflection of a version of the trial of Horatius which was conducted by quaestors).[204] Their title *prima facie* implies that their primary function was to investigate and punish crime—*quaerere* is used throughout Roman legal and literary texts in this sense—and later antiquaries rather twisted language to make the title fit their later financial functions. Zonaras (source unknown) makes the quite sensible statement that the quaestors were originally (from 509) appointed to try capital cases, whence their title, and later took over finance and eventually lost their judicial functions.[205] Varro says briefly: 'quaestores a quaerendo, qui conquirerent publicas pecunias et maleficia, quae triumviri capitales nunc conquirunt.'[206] Festus in one passage says: 'parricidi quaestores appellabantur qui solebant creari causa rerum capitalium quaerendarum', and in another very defective entry: 'quaestores . . . capitalibus unde

. . . [parri]cidi appellantur.'[207] Pomponius, a very inaccurate and muddleheaded lawyer of the second century A.D., alleges that after the creation of the censors and the aediles of the plebs financial quaestors were appointed, 'dicti ab eo quod inquirendae et conservandae pecuniae causa creati erant'; he goes on to say that 'quaestores constituebantur a populo qui capitalibus rebus praeessent: hi appellabantur quaestores parricidii, quorum etiam meminit lex duodecim tabularum'.[208] All the legal antiquaries agree that the quaestors judged capital cases in general, though sometimes called *quaestores parricidii*, and only Pomponius seems to separate financial from judicial quaestors. But the only valuable statement of Pomponius is that *quaestores parricidii* were mentioned in the Twelve Tables—whether this means that the actual title was used or that quaestors were mentioned in the context of *parricidium* or capital crime.

To these conclusions the narratives of trials conform. Trials by quaestors are recorded for *perduellio* in 486 (it was a capital offence under the Twelve Tables and no doubt before);[209] for false witness in 458;[210] for *peculatus* in 391;[211] for murder in c. 104;[212] and for an unknown crime at an unknown date (but after 243).[213] The quaestors were doubtless called *parricidii* because murder was the commonest crime they had to deal with. The quaestors who tried capital cases in historical times were two of the regular quaestors of the year; and the trial of 457 shows that the two quaestors of the year then acted. We are told that in 458 the two quaestors tried to prosecute Volscius before the people but were prevented by tribunician veto, but those of the next year succeeded.

The *duoviri perduellionis* are much more shadowy. They are recorded three times only. First there is the account by Livy of the famous trial of Horatius under King Tullus Hostilius.[214] They are not mentioned in any other account of the trial except that of Festus (who calls them plain *duoviri* and makes the charge *parricidium*),[215] and, as argued in the appendix to this chapter, were probably injected into the Horatius trial for the trial of Rabirius in 63 B.C. They appear, secondly, in one version of the trial of Manlius Capitolinus in 384, the charge being apparently *peculatus*.[216] Thirdly there is the Rabirius trial of 63, an antiquarian revival. It is implied in all the cases that they were 'created' *ad hoc*; and Dio says that it was maintained in 63 (presumably in legal and antiquarian circles) that they ought, *more maiorum*, to be elected by the people and not nominated by the praetor as in fact they were for Rabirius.[217]

It has frequently and indeed generally been argued that the criminal jurisdiction of the tribunes, which is certainly an odd phenomenon, cannot have arisen until they became acknowledged as *de facto* magistrates, at the earliest perhaps after the restoration of the tribunate in 449, and so that all early tribunician trials are bogus. A mere 'trade union leader' of the plebs could not in early days have judged anyone, much less a patrician. This is to misconceive the revolutionary character of the primitive tribunate; the tribunes were there to protect the plebs and individual plebeians against patricians and in particular the consuls. It also forgets the primitive, and continuing, sacrosanctity of the tribunes. Their power rested on the oath of the plebs that anyone who killed, assaulted or physically obstructed a tribune was *sacer*, liable to be killed at sight without bloodguilt.[218] A tribune could thus, if physically strong and courageous enough, seize a consul and hurl him over the Tarpeian rock, and anyone who resisted could be lynched without scruple by the plebeian mob. In actual fact as late as 131 B.C. the censor Metellus Macedonicus 'on returning from the Campus at mid-day, the Forum and the Capitol being empty, was dragged by the tribune C. Atinius Labeo Macerio to the Tarpeian rock to be hurled over it'; and although some of his friends rallied they could not do anything effective 'since they had no right to resist or repel a sacrosanct person'.[219] Metellus was barely saved by another tribune who was sent for and vetoed Atinius. It was therefore a gracious concession by a tribune if he allowed his proposed victim to be tried before being cast from the rock.

Now this is what Dionysius of Halicarnassus believed. He wrote up the first tribunician trial, that of Coriolanus, at immense length precisely to illustrate the constitutional issues. The account is, of course, with all its long speeches, quite imaginary, but it sets out what later antiquarians believed. The tribunes send their aediles to seize Coriolanus, but the patricians beat the aediles off and the tribunes have not the courage to seize him themselves. They of their own motion declare Coriolanus guilty of violating their sacred rights, and condemn him to death. Civil commotions threaten, and wiser patricians propose a compromise: Coriolanus will be surrendered if the tribunes, acting in the spirit of the *lex Valeria de provocatione*, give him a trial before the people. The tribunes agree, but there is a final dispute whether Coriolanus should be tried before the plebs or the *comitia centuriata* of the people; he is tried before the plebs.[220]

That there really were capital trials before the plebeian assembly earlier than 450 is suggested by the law of the Twelve Tables already quoted, forbidding 'de capite civis rogari nisi maximo comitiatu'. It is unlikely that trials were held before the *comitia curiata*—there is no hint of it in the sources—and a *comitia populi tributa* probably did not yet exist (if it ever did). The Twelve Tables therefore were probably banning tribunician capital trials before the plebeian assembly, and the curious ritual, well attested in historical times, whereby a tribune wishing to try a citizen on a capital charge 'asked for a day' from the praetor, confirms this hypothesis.

The origin of the jurisdiction of the aediles—always for a fine—is even more obscure. There were later doubts whether the plebeian aediles were sacrosanct in the same full sense as the tribunes, as they were not covered by the original oath of the plebs.[221] In 454 one consul is said to have been prosecuted by a tribune and one by an aedile (both for fines and both for military misconduct).[222] There was no reason to invent this curious distinction of offices, and it may be true. In general the jurisdiction of the aediles becomes active after the establishment of the curule aedileship in 367, and thereafter no distinction is visible between plebeian and curule aediles, who prosecute for fines only, and usually in less important, non-political cases.

When and how *provocatio* against the higher fines was introduced is also problematic. All the recorded laws *de provocatione*, from the first *lex Valeria* to the *lex Iulia*, mention only death and scourging.[223] According to tradition a law was passed by the consuls of 454, Tarpeius and Aternius, empowering all magistrates (viz. presumably quaestors as well as consuls: tribunes and aediles were hardly magistrates then) to levy fines, but fixing a maximum fine of 30 oxen plus two sheep.[224] This looks primitive, and in Varro's day a magistrate inflicting a minimum fine still said: 'unum ovem multam dico'.[225] Oxen and sheep were not long afterwards commuted at a fixed scale into *asses*, the maximum fine being 3000 *asses*.[226] There is no record at all of a law allowing higher fines or appeal against such fines, but in fact both are frequently attested. In historical times a magistrate conducting a trial before the assembly is said to *iudicare* if the case is capital but *irrogare multam* if the penalty is a fine. This suggests that while the magistrate had the legal authority to judge and condemn to death—subject of course to *provocatio*—he could only levy a fine above the maximum by a special *rogatio* on which the assembly voted. Technically no *provocatio* would seem to lie from this, but *de facto* the procedure in pecuniary cases was evidently assimilated to that in capital cases.[227]

What offences were treated in the Twelve Tables as crimes, to be judged and punished by a magistrate, and which as private wrongs for which the injured party sued the offender, is not easy to say. The distinction was not between capital and pecuniary cases: private actions, e.g. against a thief or a debtor, might give the prosecutor the right to kill or enslave a citizen,[228] while on the other hand tribunes often prosecute criminally for a fine. The issue is in fact confused by the arbitrary power the tribunes arrogated to themselves to prosecute for a fine or even the death penalty magistrates allegedly guilty of military incompetence or ill success, or of hostility to the plebs and its officers. It would appear, however, that *perduellio* was always a public crime, tried by a magistrate before the people, and so too was *peculatus*. False witness, at any rate if it had led to the death of its victim, is twice recorded to have been tried by magistrates, the quaestor in one case and a tribune in the other. The removal of crops by magic is known to have been tried by an aedile in the second century and had no doubt always been a public crime.[229] For the other capital crimes in the Twelve Tables, corruption by a judge, arson, cutting a neighbour's crops by night,[230] we have no information whether they were tried by a magistrate before the people or left to private actions by the injured parties. Even murder is a dubious case, for according to a law attributed to Numa if anyone killed a man by accident he could offer a ram to the man's agnates at a public meeting *pro capite occisi*.[231] This implies that murder was a matter to be settled between the killer and the agnates of his victim, whether by regulated vendetta or by judicial process. The latter alternative is supported by Dionysius of Halicarnassus, who represents Volscius as telling the people that he would have preferred to bring a private action against Kaeso before the consuls;[232] on the other hand, later Roman tradition believed that Tullus Hostilius tried Horatius before the people for the murder of his sister, and associated the quaestors with *parricidium*. There were perhaps two concurrent procedures, private and public, like appeal of murder and indictment for murder in English law.

It would be rash to affirm anything about the regal age. All that can be said is that 'the pontifical records declare that there was *provocatio* even from the kings, and our augural records indicate the same';[233] and that there was a firm tradition in the first century B.C. that Tullus Hostilius permitted Horatius to appeal to the people. There are various versions of the trial: in the simplest and most plausible the king himself is the judge.[234] Some apparently believed that, as in later times, quaestors acted, and according to another version, probably spurious, the judges were the *duoviri perduellionis*.[235]

Appendix to Chapter I

THE TRIAL OF RABIRIUS

For the trial (or, as will be seen, trials) of C. Rabirius in 63 B.C. there is one primary authority, Cicero in the incompletely preserved *pro C. Rabirio perduellionis reo ad Quirites oratio* and in two minor allusions, *ad Atticum* II, i, 3 and *in Pisonem* 4, and there are two secondary sources, Suetonius, *divus Iulius* 12 and Cassius Dio XXXVII, 26–8. It will be best to elicit as much information as possible from Cicero before drawing upon the secondary authors.

Cicero is clearly speaking at a *iudicium populi* conducted by the tribune of the plebs T. Labienus. The whole speech is directed against Labienus as accusing magistrate, and the case is spoken of as 'a tribuno pl. susceptam' (4). Labienus clearly presides, since he regulates the length of speeches (6). The case had begun with a *multae irrogatio* (8) on relatively trivial charges enumerated in 7–8; but it is now capital (1, 'capitis famae fortunarumque', 2, 'in discrimen capitis', 5, 'in tanta dimicatione capitis famae fortunarumque', 'vita C. Rabiri', 31, 'capitis C. Rabiri') and is mainly concerned with the death of Saturninus. It is probable that the charge was *perduellio*, as stated in the traditional title of the speech and implied in *in Pisonem* 4: 'ego in C. Rabirio perduellionis reo XL annis ante me consulem interpositam senatus auctoritatem sustinui contra invidiam atque defendi': we know from *ad Atticum* II, i, 3 that Cicero delivered only one speech *pro Rabirio*, and Cicero is presumably alluding to this speech in the *in Pisonem*. It is implied that Cicero is speaking on the final day when the voting is to take place (5). The assembly should therefore have been the *comitia centuriata* in the Campus Martius. The allusion to Labienus producing a picture of Saturninus on the *rostra* at a *contio* (25) refers to one of the three earlier sessions.

Cicero in rather vague language charges Labienus with being responsible for an earlier trial of C. Rabirius before *duoviri perduellionis* according to an ancient ritual, and claims that that trial was stopped by himself. Of Labienus he says (11) 'crucem ad civium supplicium defigi et constitui iubes', and (12) 'hic popularis a duoviris iniussu vestro non iudicari de cive Romano sed indicta causa civem Romanum capitis condemnari coegit', and (13) 'non modo suppliciis invisitatis sed etiam verborum crudelitate inaudita violare libertatem huius populi, temptare mansuetudinem, commutare disciplinam conatus es'. Labienus is also alleged to have sought out this procedure 'ex annalium monumentis atque ex regum commentariis' (15). Of his own action Cicero says that this *perduellionis iudicium* was 'sublatum' by himself (10), that he forbade the appearance of the *carnifex* in the Forum (11), and that Labienus was repulsed from his 'regal' action by his—Cicero's—*consilium*, *virtus* and *auctoritas*. How Labienus initiated the duoviral trial remains obscure, but evidently not by a plebiscite, since the trial was 'iniussu vestro'. Cicero stopped it presumably by his consular veto: he uses the word 'veto' in 11.

On what happened at that trial Cicero says that Rabirius was condemned *indicta causa*. This would be the formal condemnation before the appeal, which in the trial of Horatius (Livy I, 26), the paradigm for this one, is pronounced without previous argument. Cicero does not say that the formulae 'i, lictor, conliga manus' and 'caput obnubito, arbori infelici suspendito' were actually pronounced: the former would have been said, according to Livy, immediately after the sentence and before the appeal, the latter only after the popular vote.

Cassius Dio seems to know of only one trial, initiated by the tribune Labienus and conducted by *duoviri*. It is brought to an end by Metellus Celer, one of the praetors, hauling down the flag on the Janiculum; and Labienus, though in law entitled to renew the prosecution, does not do so. The story is muddled and inaccurate, but may contain true information, though it is difficult to assign any particular item to one trial or the other.

The incident of the flag (which Dio explains at great length) must surely be true, and probably belongs to the second trial: otherwise Cicero could hardly have avoided some complimentary remark about Metellus' decisive intervention, and could hardly have claimed to have stopped the trial himself. The device was incidentally the only way of stopping a tribunician trial, if no other tribune was willing to use his veto and no evil omen occurred. The information in Dio that a praetor, contrary to *mos maiorum*, nominated C. and L. Caesar as *duoviri* must also be true; Suetonius' statement (*div. Iul.* 12) that C. Caesar 'sorte iudex in reum ductus tam cupide condemnavit ut ad populum provocanti nihil aeque ac iudicis acerbitas profuerit' can be reconciled with Dio if one assumes that the two *duoviri* drew lots as to which should pronounce sentence.

According to Dio, Labienus initiated the whole affair by indicting (γραψάμενος) Rabirius. The word γράφεσθαι might mean *diem dicere*, and Suetonius does say that Caesar suborned someone 'qui Gaio Rabirio perduellionis diem diceret'. This phraseology and procedure, however, could only properly apply to the second, tribunician trial. But γράφεσθαι might also stand for *nomen deferre*, and this would seem to be the way Labienus initiated the first trial, by laying information of *perduellio* by Rabirius before a praetor and requesting that he take action according to the ancient *commentarii*. The praetor must have been in the plot to accept this very strange procedure and to nominate the two Caesars. There is no hint in Dio or elsewhere that the praetor in question was Metellus Celer, who on the contrary is represented as objecting to the trial as illegal, and seems from the rest of his actions to have been a good optimate. A more likely praetor would be Lentulus Sura, who later joined Catiline.

Dio, then, conflates two trials. His account is probably correct up to the crucial point of the first trial, when he says that the *duoviri* (actually one of them) condemned Rabirius and Rabirius appealed; in these statements he is supported by Suetonius. He then jumps to the end of the second trial, and says that the voting was going against Rabirius when Metellus Celer rushed to the Janiculum. Suetonius also implies that the duoviral trial reached a completion but that Rabirius was acquitted: 'ut ad populum provocanti nihil aeque ac iudicis acerbitas profuerit'. Dio's statement that Labienus could have renewed the charge appears to be correct. Under the rule cited by Cicero in *de domo*

45 he could not have brought precisely the same case; but on the precedent of Appius Claudius Pulcher he could have prosecuted the same offence for a fine.

It is tempting to believe that the 'ancient annals and commentaries of the kings' on which Labienus relied were the same as those used by Livy for his account of the trial of Horatius, which is the first and only regal comitial trial known to us: the formulae and procedure are identical in Cicero and Livy. If so it may be possible to explain the great anomaly of the Horatius trial, *viz.* that Horatius, guilty of murder, is tried by *duoviri* for *perduellio*. (It was seen at the end of Chapter I that there exist other versions of the trial which do not have this feature: there are *duoviri* but the charge is *parricidium*, or there are not *duoviri* but the King himself is judge, as would seem natural in a primitive monarchy, or there are *quaestores parricidii* in accordance with the later practice.) Whence did the charge of *perduellio* come? Caesar, who is generally believed to have inspired the trial of Rabirius, wished to demonstrate with the utmost publicity that it was illegal to kill a Roman citizen without trial even under the *senatus consultum ultimum*. A *iudicium populi* was certainly the best possible way to achieve publicity, but the difficulty was to find a defendant: the *leges de provocatione* were all directed against magistrates, and all the magistrates involved in the *s.c. ultimum* of 100 B.C. were dead, and apparently under that of 77 B.C. nobody had been executed. The only possibility was old Rabirius, who had indeed actually killed Saturninus, but had—unfortunately—been a private citizen. He could have been accused of murder, but that would have been unsatisfactory in several ways: he would have had to be tried either in the *quaestio de sicariis*, which would give much less opportunity for publicity, or before the people by a quaestor —but Caesar wanted to undertake the prosecution himself. More important still, Caesar wanted to prove that killing a citizen without trial was not merely murder but *maiestas*, or, to use the old term, *perduellio*—high treason. A charge of *perduellio* would have the advantage that it would give rise to a *iudicium populi* and the further advantage that it would be tried by *duoviri*, one of whom could, by altering their method of appointment from popular election to nomination by a friendly praetor, be guaranteed to be Caesar himself. To achieve this result involved a little manipulation of the precedents: the famous trial of Horatius for murder had to be converted into a trial for *perduellio* before *duoviri*. But the change had the great advantage of 'proving' that even under the kings killing a citizen without trial was treason, and that not only magistrates but even private citizens were liable to the charge.

Chapter 2

IUDICIA PUBLICA

In Cicero's day the terms *iudicium publicum* or *quaestio* (which was synonymous) normally denoted a permanent criminal court presided over by a praetor or *iudex quaestionis* and manned by a large jury, who gave the verdict by majority vote. Each court was established and regulated by a statute which defined the crime or group of crimes with which it dealt and laid down rules of procedure.

In one passage, however, Cicero alludes to a different type of *iudicium publicum*. Verres, he says, held a *iudicium publicum* during his urban praetorship: 'a fine was claimed before him as praetor from Q. Opimius, who was brought into court nominally because when tribune of the plebs he had interposed his veto contrary to the Cornelian law, but really because he had said something in his tribunate displeasing to some noble'. The case was hurried through in three hours, according to Cicero, and there was such indignation in the senate that it was proposed to abolish 'genus hoc totum multarum atque eius modi iudiciorum'.[1]

This *iudicium publicum* is clearly quite distinct from the familiar courts of *repetundae* or murder. The offence arises out of a constitutional, not a criminal, statute; the magistrate who takes action is the urban praetor, and he seems to have more control over the issue than the praetor of a standing criminal court. More can be learnt about this second type of *iudicium publicum* from statutes preserved in inscriptions. In the *lex Appuleia de maiestate* of 103 B.C. it is enacted that if any senator obstructs the law he shall be liable to a fine (the amount is lost); the text goes on: 'Let any magistrate who wishes exact the money. If the claimant shall so demand, let the praetor give the appropriate number of *recuperatores* and order him, if it so appears, to be condemned to the people, and cause him to be judged ('facitoque ioudicetur'). If he is condemned let him give sureties to the urban quaestor, or let him cause his property to be sequestrated'.[2] In the law on pirates of 100 B.C. there is a similar clause exacting a fine of 200,000 sesterces from persons who may obstruct the law; but in this case: 'any person who wishes, who is a freeborn citizen of this state and who is legally entitled according to this law to sue for the money and take legal proceedings, let him act and take proceedings and report the name to him who has jurisdiction concerning this . . . and let a court ('iudicium') be established and the money paid over'. And a little further on: 'the same praetor to whom application was originally made on the matter shall appoint a judge or court', if the money has not been paid.[3] A third statute, the *lex agraria* of 55 B.C., enacts a penalty of 5,000 denarii for removing boundary stones and lays down that the jurisdiction and grant of *reciperatores* shall be vested in the *curator* appointed by the law, or, if he has ceased to exist, jurisdiction and the grant of a judge shall be with the local municipal magistrates. It further lays down that the magistrate concerned may compulsorily summon up to ten witnesses.[4]

It is clear that these *iudicia publica* are closely modelled on suits of private law. The claimant goes to a praetor, who appoints a small number of *recuperatores*. The main difference is that whereas in a private action it is the injured party who must sue, here there is no injured party and either any magistrate or more commonly any citizen (not disqualified in any way) may sue. Secondly, since the penalty goes to the state, it is the state's officers, the quaestors, who exact it; and thirdly, since the matter is in the public interest, the state uses its coercive powers to call witnesses. Similar *iudicia publica* existed at municipal level and followed the same rules. In one case the right of prosecution is reserved to 'any magistrate', but it is nearly always extended to 'any citizen'; application is made to the *duoviri*, who give *reciperatores* and compulsorily summon witnesses.[5]

According to the lawyers *iudicia publica* existed *pro publica utilitate*; but this philosophical-sounding distinction is not of great practical value. As Paulus had to admit, the *actio iniuriarum* under the *lex Cornelia*, although exercised in the public interest, is nevertheless *privata*.[6] And it is difficult to see why the punishment of forgery should be in the public interest and entrusted to a *publicum iudicium* when assault and theft remain treated as private wrongs (delicts, torts). The key distinction in the eyes of Roman lawyers seems to have been that stated by Justinian, presumably echoing a classical jurist, that courts 'are called public because their execution is generally given to any member of the public';[7] though even to that principle there were anomalous exceptions, namely the *actiones populares*, which could be brought by any member of the public but nevertheless counted as suits of private law.[8] One of them, the *actio de albo corrupto*, which was the praetor's own remedy against tampering with his edict, came very close to the special kind of *iudicia publica* that has been described above.[9] Of course, that injured parties could, and it was often they who did, bring accusations in the *iudicia publica*, and were sometimes given a preference (as they might be in *actiones populares*) is not really anomalous, because they had at least as much right as any other citizen to do so.[10]

One other piece of evidence in Cicero seems to bear on the type of *iudicium publicum* discussed above. Vatinius as tribune of the plebs passed a law 'de alternis consiliis reiciendis', which apparently means that accuser and accused could each reject one jury out of three proposed. It is impossible to believe that three juries of seventy-five persons each were allotted for them to choose from. Next year Vatinius was accused before a praetor, C. Memmius, under the *lex Licinia Iunia*, which was a constitutional statute, and the formation of the court came under his own law. He had a violent dispute with Memmius, who wished to appoint the *quaesitor* by lot, whereas Vatinius insisted that he should be chosen by alternate rejection.[11] It seems that his law was ambiguous as to whether the *quaesitor* as well as the *recuperatores* should be chosen in this way. The incident reveals that *iudicia publica* of the type under discussion might be presided over by a *quaesitor*, normally appointed by lot—presumably from the general album of jurors—by the praetor concerned. The panel of *recuperatores*, also probably chosen by lot from the album with a limited right of rejection, must have been few in number if three whole panels could be offered for rejection.

Iudicia publica or *quaestiones* of this type must have existed before 122, for in the *lex Acilia de repetundis* persons 'who have been condemned in a *quaestio* or *iudicium publicum* whereby it is illegal for them to be enrolled in the senate' may not be assigned as *patroni* or placed on the panel of jurors.[12] Now prior to the *quaestio repetundarum* established by this very law there had been only one *iudicium publicum* of the 'main' or 'standard' type in existence, namely that set up by the *lex Calpurnia* of 149 and modified by the *lex Iunia*; and that *quaestio* is alluded to in different terms in another clause of the *lex Acilia*, which excludes from the jury for the case anyone who has undergone an *actio sacramento* under the Calpurnian or Junian laws.[13] The former clause, then, must relate to *iudicia publica* of the first type. They were presumably introduced to avoid the necessity of a full-dress *iudicium populi* for the exaction of a fine every time anyone contravened a statute and however trivial the contravention.

The story of *iudicia publica* of the second, the main or standard type begins with complaints of extortion, 'res repetundae', from the provinces. In 171 Spanish delegates approached the senate asking for redress from several provincial governors. The senate ordered the praetor to whom Spain had been allotted to nominate five *recuperatores* from the senate for each defendant and to assign to the complainants advocates of their choice. One defendant was acquitted and the rest went into exile.[14] As the proceedings were civil, for *pecunia capta*, they did so presumably to escape repaying the large sums due from them. Cornelius Lentulus, consul in 156, was condemned for *repetundae* under a *lex Caecilia*, probably in 154–3, when a number of other provincial governors were condemned for the same offence; it seems likely that a special court had been set up by plebiscite to deal with a group of scandalous cases.[15]

In 149 Calpurnius Piso, tribune of the plebs, set up what Cicero calls the first standing *quaestio*.[16] We know that the procedure was civil, by *actio sacramento*, and that the only penalty was simple restitution.[17] We can infer that Piso established no special praetor for his court, or Acilius would have made use of him for nominating the first panel of jurors under his own law, whereas he gave this duty to the *praetor peregrinus*,[18] who had perhaps hitherto normally been president of the court of *repetundae*, not unnaturally, since the claimants were usually foreigners.

It may be presumed that, as in later laws, in Piso's law only senators were liable to be charged. From Cicero's emphatic and repeated statement that Piso established the first standing *quaestio* it may reasonably be inferred that it was a court of the same structure as the *quaestiones* of Cicero's own day, consisting of a president (probably a praetor) and a large jury who decided the issues by a majority vote. It can also be inferred from what we are told about Gaius Gracchus' legislation that the jurors were drawn from the senate.

There are three versions of Gaius Gracchus' 'judiciary law', as it is called in our sources. According to Plutarch he passed a law adding 300 *equites* to the existing 300 senators to form a joint album from which jurors should be drawn.[19] The *Perioche* of Livy asserts that he passed a law to enrol 600 *equites* in the senate so that *equites* had twice the numerical strength of senators in the senate; it is manifestly untrue that Gracchus did this, and the passage is probably a confused variant of Plutarch's account.[20] All the other authorities say that Gracchus transferred 'the courts' from the senate to the *equites*.[21] That this is what he did in the end is clear both from later history and from the text of the law by most scholars identified with the *lex Acilia* mentioned by Cicero,[22] which was passed by M'. Acilius Glabrio, one of Gracchus' colleagues as tribune in 123 or more probably 122 B.C. This law reorganised the court of *repetundae*, and directed the *praetor peregrinus* of the current year and the praetor in charge of the court in subsequent years to choose an album of 450 jurors who had not held any magistracy up to quaestor or tribune of the plebs and were not senators or fathers, brothers or sons of senators or the named magistrates.[23] The positive qualification is missing in the text, but must, from the literary evidence, have denoted equestrian rank, whether by requiring possession (past or present) of a public horse or—as seems more probable—of a census of at least 400,000 sesterces.[24]

It is, then, certain that by the *lex Acilia* Gaius Gracchus completely excluded senators from the court of *repetundae*. But it does not follow that the law discussed in some detail by Plutarch and in a confused fashion by Livy's epitomator is a figment of their imaginations; and there are certain signs in the *lex Acilia* that some such law may have been passed. There is in the first place the curious figure of 450 for the album, which makes no sense for a homogeneous group but would be rational if the panel consisted of senators and *equites* in the proportion of 1:2 as the *Perioche* of Livy suggests. The actual figures appear to be wrong in both authors: Plutarch rightly says 300 *equites* but makes the senatorial group the whole senate, while Livy, also assuming the whole senate to be involved, gives double their number for the *equites*. So it would seem that the figure of 450 in the *lex Acilia* was taken from a previous law; and there are other signs in its drafting that it has been rather clumsily adapted from a statute in which there was a joint album of senators and *equites*.[25] It may be suggested that this earlier law was the *lex Iunia*, passed by the tribune of the plebs M. Junius, which is mentioned in the *lex Acilia* as subsequent to the *lex Calpurnia* but prior to the *lex Acilia* itself. The Junius who passed it may have been tribune in 123 and may be the M. Junius Silanus who was consul in 109.

The court of *repetundae* in this early stage of its development has a curious blend of public and private legal procedure. It is called a *quaestio* and the praetor is said to *quaerere*;[26] these are terms of criminal law. The procedure has changed from a civil *actio sacramento* as in the *lex Calpurnia* to a criminal indictment by *nominis delatio*.[27] Witnesses are compulsorily summoned on behalf of the accuser by the praetor,[28] and he enforces payment of the damages.[29] On the other hand, as in a private, civil suit it is for the injured party, not for any citizen, to bring the charge,[30] and the penalty goes not to the state but to the injured party:[31] that it is double does not at all constitute a trait of public rather than private law.[32] On the other hand again, the jury bears little resemblance either to the *recuperatores* who were an alternative to *unus iudex* of civil procedure and had been adopted for the first type of *iudicium publicum* described above, or to the assessors who advised the magistrate empowered to judge a capital case without appeal, described in the previous chapter. *Recuperatores*, unlike the jury, were few in number (five seems to have been normal), though once appointed they tried the case and delivered the verdict without interference from the magistrate who had appointed them. Assessors may have been more numerous; but they were chosen by the magistrate at his discretion, and their opinions were not binding on him: after consulting them he made his own decision. The jury is in fact something new in the

Roman legal system, and Calpurnius, if (as seems probable) he introduced it, must be credited with an innovation. He may well have been inspired by Greek jury courts, which were familiar to the Roman upper class by his time. The jury courts of Rhodes excited the admiration of a later Roman writer, and may already have won approval.[33]

C. Gracchus passed a law against judicial conspiracy, commonly known as 'ne quis iudicio circumveniatur'. It was, according to Cicero, incorporated by Sulla in the *lex Cornelia de sicariis*, and he quotes several clauses from it;[34] in the Digest title on the *lex Cornelia* other clauses are cited which clearly belong to Gracchus' law.[35] (One cannot be certain that Sulla did not 'modernize' the wording, but Cicero appears to treat the two laws as identical.) The law, which applied to senators only, laid down penalties 'if any of them should combine or conspire to the end that any person should be condemned by a *iudicium publicum*'. Other clauses penalised any senator 'who when he was a magistrate or presiding over a *publicum iudicium* caused anyone to lay a false information so that an innocent person should be tried or condemned, or who of malice gave false witness whereby anyone should be condemned on a capital charge in a *publicum iudicium*, or when he was a magistrate or *iudex quaestionis* received money in a capital case so that anyone should be accused in public law'. From this it is to be inferred that already in 122 B.C. there existed capital *iudicia publica*; apart from the specific references in surviving clauses, which might be Sullan interpolations, the inference is proved by the fact that Sulla incorporated the Gracchan law in his *lex Cornelia de sicariis*, which concerned people who secured the deaths of people. Now these *iudicia publica* obviously cannot be the first type, which dealt with statutory fines, nor can they be the *quaestio repetundarum*, which was also not a capital court. We know of no other standing *iudicium publicum* as early as this. It seems likely therefore that Gracchus was legislating for extraordinary criminal courts. It will be remembered that by another law he penalised any magistrate who condemned a Roman citizen to death without the order of the people.[36] This dealt with men like Popilius who exercised capital jurisdiction without appeal unauthorized by law or plebiscite; it was however still possible for the senate with the aid of a tribune to procure a plebiscite authorising a capital court without appeal. Gracchus could hardly object to that procedure, but he endeavoured to secure that in future such courts should not be used for putting to death personal or political enemies.

It is not easy to determine the structure of those extraordinary courts from the surviving clauses, particularly as their wording may have been modified by Sulla to fit contemporary conditions. They might have been 'old style' courts consisting of a magistrate with assessors or 'new style' courts consisting of a magistrate with a jury. Neither jurors nor assessors are specifically mentioned, but either would be covered by the clause against combination and conspiracy. In Cicero's day a juror who voted corruptly for a capital condemnation came under the law.[37] The phrase '. . . who was a magistrate or presided over a *iudicium publicum*' perhaps suggests a jury court, but the second part of it may be a Sullan addition, as may be 'iudexve quaestionis' in another clause. The procedure was probably inquisitorial, for no mention is made of a false accuser, only of one who lays false information. It is clear that only senators manned these courts, otherwise Gracchus would not have confined the penalties to senators.

The history of the courts for the next forty years is most obscure. Our authorities are interested only in the political question, whether the jurors were senators or *equites*, and do not record the establishment of any new courts: on the contrary, they assume the existence of several courts from the beginning, and attribute the periodic changes in the status required for jury service to 'judiciary laws' covering all the courts. They are proved wrong in this assumption in the case of Gaius Gracchus, where the surviving text of the *lex Acilia* shows that his law was not a judiciary law but a law of extortion which incorporated new rules on the selection of the jury: they may be equally wrong about their later 'judiciary laws'.

In 116 B.C. Marius was accused of electoral corruption (*ambitus*) and only just acquitted by a tie in the votes of the judges.[38] This strongly suggests the existence of a *quaestio ambitus*, but it is not conclusive. Livy and his epitomator refer to two bribery laws in the first half of the second century (181 and 159), but none thereafter.[39] These laws cannot have set up a *quaestio ambitus*, since Piso's *quaestio repetundarum* was the first of its kind. There may, of course, have been unrecorded bribery laws between 149 and 116, but it is perhaps more probable that

Marius was tried by a special court set up by the senate, or that the court which tried him was a *iudicium publicum* of the first type and the judges in the story *recuperatores*.

There follow two special courts. In 113 Cassius Longinus was appointed by plebiscite to investigate the alleged violation of the chastity of the Vestal Virgins. He condemned several persons to death: the procedure was accusatorial, by *nominis delatio*, and there was a jury.[40] In 110 the tribune Mamilius set up a court by plebiscite to investigate alleged corruption of senators by Jugurtha; this court was presided over by three *quaesitores* and had a jury of 'Gracchan judges'—presumably drawn from the annual album of 450.[41]

In 106 the consul Q. Servilius Caepio passed a law, which Cicero once describes as 'iudiciaria',[42] whereby jury service was either entirely transferred from *equites* to senators or shared between the two orders.[43] This change was short-lived, for, probably in 101, Servilius Glaucia, tribune of the plebs, restored the courts to the *equites*.[44] References to these two *leges Serviliae* are not always easy to disentangle. Cicero says that the rule whereby money could be recovered not only from the condemned person but also from third parties to whom it had passed was enacted not only in the *lex Iulia* but in the *lex Cornelia* and before that in the *lex Servilia*;[45] this must refer to Glaucia's law, the immediate predecessor of Sulla's, and shows that Glaucia's law was, like the other two, a *lex repetundarum*. In another passage he says that successful accusers of Latin status were rewarded with Roman citizenship 'by the very severe Servilian law', which was promoted by 'the leading men of the state and the most responsible and prudent citizens'.[46] Cicero would hardly have used such language of Glaucia and the *populares*, so this reference is probably to Caepio's law. In that case his law too must have been a *lex repetundarum*, for Latins receive citizenship in the *lex Acilia* and so far as we know it was only for *repetundae* that Latins and other aliens could bring an accusation. Cicero gives clear information that it was Glaucia's law that introduced *comperendinatio*;[47] it was probably also his law that made the extortion court into a *iudicium publicum* in the full sense by opening up the right of accusation to all citizens. The *lex Acilia*, which no doubt followed the *lex Calpurnia* on the point, had the rule that only injured parties could accuse, and if there were several of them they apparently made a joint charge presented by one advocate.[48] (The only possible case which conflicts with this rule is that of M'. Aquillius, who was tried, probably in 126 B.C., for receiving bribes from King Mithridates and others in connexion with his settlement of the new province of Asia—in particular for ceding Phrygia Major to Mithridates. Cicero states that at this trial the accuser was P. Lentulus, *princeps senatus*, and his *subscriptor* C. Rutilius Rufus.[49] The case could indeed come under the definition of *res repetundae*, but it was primarily a political offence, and it seems likely that the senate, which drastically overhauled the whole settlement, set up a special court to try Aquillius.) Now if any citizen might accuse, several might wish to do so and a choice had to be made between them. This was done by *divinatio*, a preliminary hearing before a jury. In his *divinatio* against Caecilius, Verres' quaestor, Cicero cites other cases of *repetundae* where the accused governor's quaestor had been rejected as accuser: they are the attempted accusations of L. Flaccus, governor of Asia, probably about 92, by M. Aurelius Scaurus; of C. Servilius, governor of Sicily in 102, by L. Philo; and of T. Albucius, governor of Sardinia probably about 102, by Cn. Pompeius Strabo.[49a] Cicero apparently knows of no earlier cases; it thus looks as if it was under the *lex Servilia* of Glaucia that charges of *repetundae* could first be brought by any citizen.

Either in his first tribunate, 103, or in his second, 100, Saturninus passed a *lex Appuleia de maiestate*,[50] which redefined the charge of treason and almost certainly established a *iudicium publicum* to try it; the trial of Norbanus for *maiestas*, probably in 95, was before a *quaestio* with equestrian jurors.[51] This *quaestio maiestatis* was the first *iudicium publicum* to try capital cases. There was, of course, no *provocatio ad populum* against its sentences any more than there had been against special courts established by law or plebiscite in earlier times; for by the *lex Appuleia* the people had ordered the successive praetors or *iudices quaestionis* to conduct a capital investigation. (It was left for M. Antonius, not a great constitutional lawyer, to enact that the *quaestiones* of *maiestas* and *vis* should be subject to *provocatio*.)[52]

Sometime in these years a third *iudicium publicum* was created, that for murder (*de sicariis*). There had, of course, been special murder courts before, the latest recorded being that presided over by the praetor Tubulus in 142 and that conducted by the consuls in 138 for the Sila murders. The latter was certainly an old-fashioned *quaestio* by two magistrates sitting with assessors, and the same is no doubt true of the former.[53] Nor does it appear to have been a permanent murder court over which Cassius Longinus presided in the years before 113 B.C. According to Asconius, 'whenever he was *quaesitor* of any court in which enquiry was made about a death he used to urge the judges and almost dictate to them . . . that investigation be made into who profited by the death of him whose death was under enquiry'.[54] These courts, then, had juries, but were evidently set up *ad hoc* to investigate important murders, and operated inquisitorially without an accuser. As for *iudicia populi* for murder, the last recorded was held by the quaestor Pompeius in about 103.[55] On the other hand there was certainly a murder court in existence before Sulla's *lex Cornelia de sicariis et veneficis*. Cicero, speaking in 80 B.C., talks as if the *quaestio de sicariis* had been in existence for some time, at any rate before the civil war, and cites a case which had been tried by a jury some years ago.[56] There is an inscription which puts the date still further back: C. Claudius Pulcher is recorded to have been in succession curule aedile, *iudex quaestionis veneficis*, and then *praetor repetundis*. He is known to have been aedile in 99, and must have been president of the murder court shortly afterwards—next year, if later practice was followed.[57]

A court for *peculatus* was also created about this time. The young Gnaeus Pompeius was tried before it in 86, and acquitted by the jury.[58]

As there were, by 91 B.C., three or four *iudicia publica* in existence, two of them certainly and all of them probably with equestrian juries, it is probable that the measure proposed by Livius Drusus, tribune of the plebs in that year, was—as Livy's epitomator states—a *lex iudiciaria*, dealing with the composition of the juries in all the courts. Our authorities differ as to the nature of the proposal: according to Appian it was to add 300 *equites* to the senate and take jurors from this enlarged body, while the Livian version is that he proposed to share the juries equally between senators and *equites*.[59] The latter version must be right, because Drusus also proposed to set up a new *quaestio* for judicial corruption, to which *equites* as well as senators would be liable.[60] Drusus' laws, if passed, were forthwith annulled, so that the courts remained in the hands of equestrian jurors. In the same year the Social War broke out, and the tribune Q. Varius passed a law setting up a special court to try persons alleged to have had treasonable relations with the Italian allies; it had an equestrian jury. All the other courts were suspended during the Social War, but the *quaestio Variana* went on;[61] the composition of its juries was, however, altered in 89 by the tribune Plautius Silvanus: under his law each of the thirty-five tribes elected fifteen persons without regard to whether they were senators, *equites*, or mere plebeians.[62] This system does not seem to have applied to the other courts when they were revived.

Sulla in his dictatorship entirely remodelled the whole system of courts. He enacted new statutes for the existing courts of extortion, treason, murder and (probably) peculation, namely the *leges Corneliae repetundarum*, *maiestatis*, *de sicariis et veneficis* and *peculatus*. What revisions he made we do not know, except that he incorporated Gracchus' law on judicial conspiracy into his law of murder. He set up what appear to be two new courts, for electoral corruption and for forgery (originally testamentary forgery) and coining, by the *leges Corneliae de ambitu* and *testamentaria* or *de falsis*. He also passed a *lex Cornelia de iniuriis* which dealt with assault and housebreaking and apparently set up a jury court—a clause of the law is quoted which excludes all near relatives by blood or marriage of the prosecutor from serving as *iudices*, which must mean jurors. It appears, however, that only an injured party could prosecute, and the classical jurists speak of the action as being 'mixto iure' or private, despite its being tried before a jury. Finally, having doubled the senate by the enrollment of 300 *equites*, Sulla enacted that juries should be drawn from the senate.[63] This arrangement lasted only about ten years, for in 70 B.C. the praetor Aurelius Cotta passed a law whereby juries were drawn equally from senators, *equites* and *tribuni aerarii*. The latter are often addressed as *equites* by Cicero, and were probably men of much the same social class with a lower property qualification. Cotta's law was thus a victory for the equestrian order, who in effect secured two thirds of the places.[64] This arrangement was not disturbed by Pompey in 55, for his *lex Pompeia* merely enacted that the richest men within each class should be selected,[65] nor even in the special album of jurors which he set up in 52.[66] It was evidently considered political dynamite to upset Cotta's compromise, which lasted until Julius Caesar in his dictatorship removed the *tribuni aerarii*.[67]

More courts were established from time to time. In 78 the consul Lutatius Catulus passed a *lex Lutatia de vi* under which a court was established,[68] and at an uncertain date before 63 a second statute on violence, the *lex Plautia de vi*, was passed. It did not supersede the *lex Lutatia*, which was still in force when Cicero pleaded for Caelius in 56, but it had its own separate *quaestio*: presumably the two laws somehow dealt with different types of violence.[69] The law *de vi* passed by Pompey in his third consulship had only temporary application, being limited to the death of Clodius and the disorders which followed; the *leges Lutatia* and *Plautia* were probably superseded by the *lex Iulia de vi* —or perhaps the *leges Iuliae de vi publica* and *privata*—enacted by Caesar in his dictatorship.[70]

The *lex Cornelia de ambitu* was superseded in 67 by a *lex Calpurnia*, which added a fine to Sulla's penalty of ten years' exclusion from office and the senate;[71] and this in turn was replaced in 63 by Cicero's own *lex Tullia*, which increased the penalty to ten years' exile, and now for the first time made exile a formal penalty of the criminal law.[72] In 55 B.C. Crassus in his second consulship passed a yet more severe law against organised electoral corruption, the *lex Licinia de sodaliciis*. It did not replace the *lex Tullia*, but had its own court, which was of a peculiar structure.[73] Pompey in his third consulship of 52 passed a *lex Pompeia de ambitu*, stiffening the penalties and making the procedure of the court more rigorous. It was retrospective back to 70 B.C.; and it was apparently still in force in 45 when Sestius was tried under it.[74]

Julius Caesar as consul in 59 enacted a *lex Iulia de repetundis* and in his dictatorship a *lex Iulia maiestatis* which replaced Sulla's laws.[75] Pompey, probably in his second consulship, passed a *lex Pompeia de parricidio* reinstating the gruesome old punishment for parricide.[76] Caelius in 50 B.C. alludes to a criminal court held under a *lex Scantinia*, which apparently dealt with sexual offences;[77] and in 63 B.C. Cicero mentions a *lex Fabia* which enacted penalties for the kidnapping of slaves or free citizens: the imperial lawyers regard the *lex Fabia* as one of the *leges iudiciorum publicorum*, and it therefore presumably established a *quaestio*.[78]

Certain *ad hoc* courts need also to be mentioned. In 95 B.C. the *lex Licinia Mucia* ordered all Italians to be sent to their own cities and established a jury court for trying contested claims to citizenship, and in 65 B.C. C. Papius, tribune of the plebs, passed a similar law establishing a similar court,[79] which this time became a standing jurisdiction. In 61, when Clodius was accused of violating the mysteries of the *Bona Dea*, a special court was required to try him *de incestu*, as the offence was not covered by any statute. The consuls with the approval of the senate promulgated a bill that a praetor should preside and select the jury from the existing album; but one of the tribunes threatened to veto the bill and promulgated another whereby the jury was chosen by lot in the ordinary way.[80] When Clodius had been murdered in 52 by Milo, Pompey as sole consul passed a law *de vi*, already mentioned, specifically dealing with the murder and the subsequent riots. The law provided that a *quaesitor* of consular standing be elected, and enabled Pompey to select a special album of 360 jurors; it also enacted a special procedure for trials under it.[81]

Under the *lex Acilia* a praetor has charge of the court for extortion;[82] a *praetor repetundis* is first recorded in 95 B.C. in *I.L.S.* 45. The *lex Appuleia de maiestate*, on the other hand, speaks of a *iudex* to be appointed under the law,[83] and C. Claudius Pulcher, the *praetor repetundis* is the above-mentioned inscription, was *iudex quaestionis veneficis* a few years earlier. With only six praetors, much in demand for the provinces, it was difficult to spare more than one for the criminal courts, and ex-aediles were therefore used as *iudices quaestionum*. When Sulla increased the number of praetors to eight and they no longer went out to provinces during their year of office it was possible for praetors to preside over all the six courts: in 80 we find the praetor Fannius in charge of the despised murder court.[84] But the number of statutory courts soon began to increase, with one and then two *de vi*, another *de plagiariis* under the *lex Fabia*, another on disputed citizenship, another *de sodaliciis* and yet another under the *lex Scantinia* for sexual offences: six in all. It was moreover found necessary to have more than one court for murder: in 66 we find two *de sicariis* and a third *de veneficis*.[85]

It thus became increasingly necessary once again to use *iudices quaestionum*. These were, in all cases where we have enough information to determine their standing, ex-aediles in the year following their magistracy;[86] but with only four aediles a year there would not always have been enough men of this standing, and perhaps they had to serve a second year. The procedure seems to have been that the senate each year decided which of the courts should be praetorian provinces, and naturally assigned to the praetors the politically important courts: *repetundae*, *ambitus*, *sodalicia*, *maiestas*, *peculatus*. The praetors designate then drew lots for the court which each should take, together with the two great civil jurisdictions, *urbana* and *peregrina*. The aediles (and perhaps ex-aediles) would then draw lots for the less attractive courts for murder, violence, forgery and the like.[87] The *iudices quaestionum* had precisely the same duties and powers as the praetors: they could receive or reject charges, conduct the *subsortitio*—and presumably the initial *sortitio*—of jurors, exercise disciplinary authority over jurors, and they were attended by *scribae* and lictors. They had to swear to the statute under which they held their court, and were liable to penalties for corruption in their court.[88]

A praetor or *iudex quaestionis* normally presided over one court for a year; most of the apparent exceptions can be straightforwardly accounted for. In 56 B.C. Sestius was accused *de vi* before the praetor M. Aemilius Scaurus, but in the same year Caelius was tried *de vi* before a certain Cn. Domitius, while one Cn. Domitius was *praetor ambitus*. Caelius was tried again *de vi* two years later before a Domitius. There is no difficulty about there being two courts *de vi* in 56: Caelius was tried under the *lex Lutatia*, Sestius presumably under the *lex Plautia*. The three Domitii cannot all be identical, and the simplest solution is to postulate that one was *praetor ambitus* in 56, the other *iudex quaestionis de vi* in 56 and *praetor de vi* in 54.[89] In 52 again there were two *quaesitores de vi* besides the special consular under the *lex Pompeia*, Domitius Ahenobarbus. One of them, C. Considius, is stated to have been under the *lex Plautia*; the other, L. Fabius, was presumably under the *lex Lutatia*.[90] For 54 B.C. there is a more intractable problem. In this year C. Alfius Flavus is called *quaesitor* both in the court *de sodaliciis* and in that *de maiestate*, while a praetor, Servilius, is president of the court *de sodaliciis*. One must presume that Alfius Flavus was president of the court of *maiestas* and Servilius of that *de sodaliciis* (the latter certainly, the former possibly as praetor), and that Alfius was directed to take on the court *de sodaliciis* temporarily because Servilius was ill or otherwise incapacitated.[91]

When there was only one *iudicium publicum*, that for *repetundae*, it was natural that the praetor in charge of it should select the album of jurors from which its juries should be drawn; and that is what the *lex Acilia* laid down. The praetor was at the beginning of each year to choose 450 persons, with whatever qualification it was (past or present tenure of a public horse or a property of 400,000 sesterces),[92] between the ages of 30 and 60, excluding senators and those who had held any magistracy up to tribune of the plebs or quaestor, and the sons, fathers or brothers of the above, excluding also gladiators, those condemned by a *publicum iudicium* whereby they were excluded from the senate, and those overseas or not having a Roman domicile. The praetor was required to post up his list in a public place and cause it to be read aloud at a public meeting, and to swear an oath that he had chosen the best men as jurors.[93] By the end of the century, when several *iudicia publica* had been set up, some changes must have been made, but we have no information on the subject. It may be presumed that juries for all the cour s were drawn from a common album, perhaps enlarged from the 450 of the *lex Acilia*, and that the selection of the panel will have been transferred to some magistrate not connected with any of the courts: the obvious choice would be the urban praetor, and in fact he it is who performs this function in 66 B.C. and has apparently been performing it for a considerable time.[94]

Under the *lex Acilia* the album consisted of 450 *equites*. From Sulla's dictatorship it consisted solely of senators; the number available after deducting magistrates and those 'absentes rei publicae causa' cannot have been much over 450. The album was divided into *decuriae* (it is not known how many, or how large they were), and each jury was apparently allotted from one decury.[95] From 70 B.C. the album consisted of equal numbers of senators, *equites* and *tribuni aerarii*, and these groups were now called decuries.[96] We happen to know that the senatorial section numbered 300,[97] and the total number must therefore have been 900; they are perhaps identical with the 'nongenti' who checked the voting and counting at the *comitia*.[98] The urban praetors had full discretion in selecting jurors for the album (except for limited categories like those set out in the *lex Acilia*); they could even select men who had received a censorial mark of disgrace.[99] They were accused of exploiting their powers as a form of patronage, enrolling their own protégés and people who were for financial reasons anxious to serve.[100] Pompey in his second consulship tried to improve the quality of jurors by enacting that the wealthiest members of each category should be nominated and that they should be obliged to serve.[101] In his third consulship he selected a special panel of 360 for his court *de vi*; they were chosen from the same three orders.[102] Julius Caesar abolished the panel of *tribuni aerarii*, and Antony substituted for it one of centurions.[103]

The *lex Acilia* had as its rule that only injured parties were allowed to accuse. The right to do so seems to have been extended to all Roman citizens under Glaucia's law of extortion,[104] but injured peregrines did not thereby apparently lose their previous right: under Augustus and his successors they could certainly accuse, and Caelius, describing the trial of Claudius Pulcher, proconsul of Asia, for extortion in 51, mentions that a certain Pausanias, whose *patronus* he was, had made an application to the praetor to bring a subsidiary charge against M. Servilius as having received part of the extorted money. Pausanias was clearly the principal, and was presumably the representative of the province.[105] Under the *lex Papia* on citizenship also it was possible for a foreigner to bring an accusation. Balbus' accuser was a fellow-Gaditane who had failed to establish his claim to Roman citizenship; and Cicero mentions a case in which the city of the Mamertines had accused one of their own citizens, and envisages the possibility that Gades might do the same.[106] Otherwise it appears that accusers had to be Roman citizens. Certain categories of persons were debarred: Cicero speaks of 'laws in which it is laid down for what reasons a person may not hold a magistracy or be selected as a juror or accuse another person'.[107] Most of our information comes from the classical jurists, but many of the rules they give were no doubt of republican origin. Women and minors might not accuse except when they were personally interested: they could, for instance, accuse the alleged murderer of a relative or the forger of a will affecting their interests. Freedmen could not accuse their patrons, nor sons their parents. Gladiators, actors and procurers were excluded. Persons condemned in a *iudicium publicum* were excluded, as were those convicted of *calumnia* or *praevaricatio* or of accepting money for making or refraining from an accusation, or of giving false evidence.[108]

The motives of accusers were, of course, various. In the courts of murder and forgery it was no doubt usually an injured party who brought the accusation, and the same must often have been true for *ambitus* and *sodalicia*. Murena was accused by his unsuccessful competitor Sulpicius, and Plancius similarly by Laterensis. Young men sought to make themselves a name in the political world by the successful prosecution of one of their elders. Political enemies tried to break each other's careers by securing their condemnation in the courts. There were also accusers whose motive was the reward offered by law for a condemnation: when Milo was accused *de vi* under the *lex Pompeia* and it was confidently believed that he would be condemned, he was promptly accused of *ambitus*, *sodalicia* and *vis* (under another statute) in the anticipation that he would be unable to appear and would be condemned in absence, as actually happened. One of the accusers, the *nobilis* Appius Claudius, refused the reward, but the others took theirs.[109] Accusers such as this were commonly called *quadruplatores*, and held in low esteem by the politicians.[110] Others again made accusations with the object of cutting out serious accusers and procuring an acquittal by deliberately bungling the case: the most famous instance is Caecilius, Verres' quaestor. Finally there were doubtless some who acted out of genuine public spirit.

There was nothing to prevent an accused person from making an accusation while his own trial was pending or even in progress. A striking case is that of Scaurus, who was accused of extortion by Caepio and himself accused Caepio on the same charge; by asking for a shorter period for collecting evidence he got his case priority on the list—and won it.[111] Another less successful attempt was that of Sempronius Rufus, who accused his accuser Tuccius of *vis* when his own trial was well under way and got special priority ('extraordinarius reus') for his case. But he not only failed to get a conviction but was himself found guilty of *calumnia*.[112] Even condemned persons might in some circumstances be given special leave to make accusations. Cicero records a case in which persons convicted of electoral corruption were allowed by a jury (presumably that of the *divinatio*) to bring a charge under the same law.[113]

Under the *lex Acilia* the first stage in an action was *nominis delatio* before the praetor, who forthwith exacted an oath against *calumnia* (that is that the accuser was not bringing a false charge out of malice) and assigned him advocates and made arrangements for empanelling a jury.[114] In the later *iudicia publica*, when several accusers might appear, the procedure was necessarily more complicated. It began with *postulatio*, or in full 'nominis delationem postulare', an application for leave to accuse.[115] The praetor could turn down the application for a variety of reasons. The accuser might be disqualified on one of the grounds mentioned above. The charge might not be in accordance with the law: before Caesar was *iudex de sicariis* in 64 presidents of that court had rejected charges of murder against those who had killed citizens in the Sullan proscriptions on the ground that they enjoyed an amnesty under the Cornelian Laws.[116] The accused might also be legally immune from prosecution: the *lex Acilia* expressly exempted the magistrate in his year of office, and this rule became general—Clodius, for example, evaded an accusation of *vis* by Milo by getting himself elected aedile just in time.[117] Not long afterwards (before 113 B.C.) a *lex Memmia* extended exemption to all 'absentes rei publicae causa'. So a man in danger of prosecution might evade it by getting a friend to nominate him as a *legatus*. But in this the praetor of a court seems to have had some discretion: in 54 the praetor *de sodaliciis* ordered C. Messius, nominated legate to Caesar, to return and stand his trial, and Messius obeyed.[118] On the other hand M. Antonius, quaestor of Asia in 113, summoned home by L. Cassius the 'scopulus reorum' to stand trial on the charge of violating the chastity of a Vestal Virgin, is said to have had the legitimate protection of the *lex Memmia* but to have scorned it, returned, and been acquitted.[119]

After the *postulatio* it must be presumed that the praetor named a day within which other persons might make a similar request. If others applied he empanelled a jury for the *divinatio*,[120] to decide which should have the right of accusing and who should be his supporting speakers (*subscriptores*). An accuser might act alone, but this was unusual; he normally brought with him one, two, or even three *subscriptores*. The jury for this purpose sat unsworn and merely heard speeches by contestants: no evidence was heard or documents produced. The jury normally selected one of the accusers, with the *subscriptores* he had chosen, but it was free to assign one of the rejected accusers as *subscriptor* to his successful rival.[121]

After the *lex Acilia* we hear no more of the praetor assigning *patroni* (advocates) to accusers. In most cases the accuser made the charge on his own initiative and was confident of ability to conduct his case; if he distrusted his powers he could enlist *subscriptores* of his choice. Even if a foreigner or foreign community wished to bring a charge of *repetundae* or the like they usually, it would seem, chose a *patronus* for themselves, and he made the formal charge in his own name, with *subscriptores*. In such a case (it happened to Cicero in the Verrine case)[122] he might have to undergo a *divinatio*, and the provincial community might find themselves saddled with an accuser they had not chosen. It seems, however, to have been still possible for a foreign accuser to apply to the court for counsel: this was certainly the rule under the principate,[123] and it may have been in this way that Caelius became *patronus* of the province of Asia in its case against Appius Claudius.[124] Defendants made their own arrangements. There was no limit to the number of *patroni* they could brief until Augustus fixed a maximum: Scaurus in 54 B.C. created a precedent by having six; the number hitherto had rarely exceeded four. In the last years of the Republic and the Triumvirate the number sometimes rose to twelve.[125]

The next process was *nominis delatio*, the making of the formal charge, and its acceptance by the praetor, *nominis receptio*. The charge had to be made in writing; the set form used under the *lex Iulia de adulteriis*, quoted by Paulus, is no doubt standard: 'Date. Before *x*, praetor. Lucius Titius has declared that he charges Maevia under the Julian law of adultery, because he says that she has committed adultery with Gaius Seius in the city of *x*, house of *x*, on such-and-such date'.[126] How much detail was required under other laws is not known. Cicero in his opening speech against Verres merely states 'that he has illegally taken 40 million sesterces from Sicily', and Asconius gives the charge against Saufeius under the *lex Plautia de vi* as succinctly: '. . . that he has occupied strong points and carried a weapon'.[127] The written charge, or *inscriptio*, was signed by the accuser and his *subscriptores*. They also took an oath against *calumnia*, which is laid down in the *lex Acilia*[128] and was no doubt the general rule, and doubtless also against *praevaricatio*, as in imperial times, in the form that they 'will press this charge and will persevere in the accusation until sentence is given'.[129] The accused had to be summoned to the *nominis delatio*, and Cicero implies that it was illegal for his name to be received in his absence.[130] This rule presumably did not apply to contumacious absence but to cases where the accused was abroad and had not received adequate notice. But there seems in fact to be no recorded case of contumacious absence from *nominis delatio*: Antonius and Messius, as we saw, duly returned—though Antonius had a legitimate claim to stay away—and Milo, when prosecuted ('postulatus') for *ambitus* and *sodalicia* and summoned by the presidents of those two courts, made an appearance and asked for his trial to be postponed until after his trial for *vis*. Having been condemned for *vis* he was then condemned in both the other courts.[131] We have therefore no direct evidence of what happened if an accused man did refuse to respond to the praetor's summons, but he could presumably in such a case be arrested and held, in the same way that Vettius the informer, having admitted before the senate that he had carried a weapon, was ordered by *senatus consultum* to be put in chains and was subsequently tried *de vi*.[132] It was possible, on the rather doubtful authority of a scholiast,[133] for the accused to plead guilty forthwith at this stage by making no response to the charge; but we know of no case when an accused man did thus plead guilty.

The next business was the *inquisitio*. Under the *lex Acilia* the accuser may ask for a period in which to collect evidence in Italy or overseas, and the praetor may assign him as many days for this as he thinks fit. The accuser may also ask for up to forty-eight witnesses to be summoned, and the praetor can issue a summons (*testimonium denuntiare*) to as many as he thinks fit.[134] There are similar provisions for the summons of witnesses in the agrarian law of 55 B.C., the charter of Urso, and the edict of Augustus on the aqueduct of Venafrum;[135] so it may be presumed that they were common form. In the Ciceronian age the accuser had authority from the praetor to summon witnesses and impound documents himself.[136] In most cases, it would seem, ten days was considered a sufficient interval for *inquisitio*,[137] but in cases of *repetundae*,[138] where evidence had to be gathered from overseas, longer periods could be allowed. M. Scaurus, governor of

Sardinia and Corsica, received thirty days for each island, and Cicero asked for 110 days for Sicily (which he calls a very meagre period), though he actually only spent fifty days there.[139] When the praetor allotted thirty days to Vatinius this was not for an ordinary trial but for a *multae petitio* under the *lex Licinia Iunia*, which had laid down that period.[140] *Inquisitio* could be exploited by ingenious defendants to postpone or even avoid trial. The elder Scaurus, as we saw,[141] when Caepio accused him of *repetundae*, counter-attacked by accusing his accuser of the same offence and taking a shorter period for *inquisitio*, so that Caepio's trial came on before his own. Verres also played for time very neatly by putting up an accuser to charge a senator with *repetundae* in Achaea and ask for 108 days' *inquisitio*. This trial, therefore, came up before that of Verres, occupying the attention of the *repetundae* court; and it was spun out over three months.[142]

Under the Acilian rules the praetor causes the jury to be empanelled immediately after the *nominis delatio* and assignment of advocates, and apparently uses it to advise him on the period to allow for *inquisitio* and the number of witnesses to be summoned.[143] It was no doubt found that this arrangement facilitated corruption and intimidation of the jury, and by the post-Sullan period juries were empanelled after the *inquisitio* and shortly before the trial was due to come on; it might not actually do so for weeks or months later if another case was in progress in the same court. The jury for Verres' trial was empanelled after Cicero had returned from Sicily, some time before the consular elections (about the middle of July), that is a month or more before the trial actually began on 5 August.[144] This was presumably because it could not be foreseen when the Achaean trial would end and a jury had to be in being for Verres' case to start at any time.

The choice of jurors under the Acilian provisions was as follows: after the defendant had produced a list of all persons on the album related to him by blood or marriage or membership of the same *sodalitas* or *collegium*, and all these having been set aside, the accuser nominated 100 persons from the remainder and the defendant chose 50 out of those 100. If the accused failed to play his part the accuser was entitled simply to nominate the 50 jurors, omitting relatives or associates of the accused to the best of his knowledge and belief.[145] This system of nominated jurors (*iudices editicii*) evidently favoured prosecutors and was strongly disliked by defendants. It appears to have been modified a little to be less prejudicial to defendants, probably by Glaucia; for Cicero speaks of a time when, the jury being all *equites*, 125 were nominated and 75 could be rejected by the defendant, again leaving 50.[146] In some courts *editicii iudices* were still empanelled under their statutes in Cicero's day. In his speech for P. Sulla, who was tried *de vi* (it is not known under which statute), Cicero speaks of the jury as 'having been chosen by the accusers in the hope that they will be severe'.[147] Under the *lex Licinia de sodaliciis* the accuser chose four of the thirty-five tribes; of those the defendant might reject one and the accuser could then choose the jurors from the remaining three—not from those on the album but from the whole membership of those tribes. The defendant could not challenge any individual juror, though Cicero mentions that in a recent case the jury had consented to five of their number being rejected.[148] Charges of organized judicial corruption were no doubt very difficult to prove, but the dice certainly seem to have been heavily loaded against the defendant. According to Cicero the intention of the senate when they discussed the bill had been that the accuser should choose the four tribes in which bribery had been most rife, so that the jurors should be both witnesses and judges; if so, the intention was not fulfilled: accusers naturally picked tribes in which the defendant was unpopular. In the speech for Roscius of Ameria, accused of parricide under the *lex Cornelia de sicariis*, Cicero says of the jury: 'You have been chosen from the city for the senate for your dignity, from the senate for this jury for your severity.'[149] The jurors in this case had been selected, but apparently not by the accuser but by a magistrate. This may have been a special provision under the law for cases of parricide, for ordinary murder was tried by a normal jury.

In the Verres case, which was *de repetundis*, Cicero expressly mentions that the jury was selected by lot (*sortitio*) and that vacancies would also have been filled by lot (*subsortitio*).[150] In the Oppianicus case (*de veneficis*) vacancies were filled by lot, and it may be presumed that the original jury was so appointed.[151] These cases both fell before 70 B.C.; but by 57, as will presently be seen, all trials could be held up if the sortition of jurors was prevented. In a *subsortitio* the urban praetor and the praetor of the court concerned both played a part. The *iudex quaestionis* Junius was held responsible for improper *subsortitiones* to his jury, but Verres as urban praetor is said to have actually drawn the lots and made the record in his books.[152] In the initial allotment of a jury the quaestors (presumably the urban quaestors) also took some part: this emerges from the manoeuvres by which Clodius succeeded in holding up his trial for *vis* in December 57. He prevented the elections of aediles and quaestors from taking place, so that when the quaestors of the year went out of office on 5 December no juries could be empanelled. Metellus Nepos, one of the consuls, who favoured Clodius, ordered the praetor to accept no accusation before jurors could be allotted, but a consul elect, Marcellinus, announced in the senate that he would himself allot the jurors through the urban praetor, and when the allotment had been made the elections would be held: anyone who held up the courts would be acting against the public interest. Evidently Clodius got his way in the end: the aedilician elections were held first and he was himself elected, thus becoming immune from prosecution; then the quaestors were elected and the courts could reopen.[153] It seems likely from all this that the urban praetor actually drew the names for a jury; the urban quaestor made an official record of the names; but the president of the court was nevertheless, as has been said, responsible for taking on an improperly drawn jury: it was apparently held the fault of Domitius, the *praetor de vi*, that he had too few jurors when Caelius' trial came on.[154]

In the period from 81 to 70 B.C. a jury was drawn from one of the *decuriae* into which the album of senators was divided. Both sides then had the right of rejecting a limited number of jurors. According to Cicero non-senators could reject only three; it is not stated how many senators could reject, but Verres is known to have turned down six.[155] It is not clear whether, if one party was a senator and the other not, the senator could reject six or more and the non-senator only three; Sulla was quite capable of enacting so unfair a rule, but it may be that the limitation to three only applied if both parties were commoners. Juries at that period were necessarily small, since the album cannot have been much over 450. In the trial of Verres Cicero can speak of the jury being 'almost wholly transformed' by the change of eight jurors, and in the Oppianicus case only thirty-two jurors voted.[156]

A clause of the *lex Acilia* lays down that the same jury, once empanelled, must continue to serve till the conclusion of the case.[157] This continued to be the rule, but individual jurors might, of course, cease in the course of the trial to be able to serve, by death or illness or because the proceedings went on into the next year and they entered upon office as magistrates. Such gaps were filled by *subsortitio*; it would be natural to assume that the supplementary jurors would have to come from the same decury as the other jurors, and that would be the best explanation of Cicero's charge that in the trial of Oppianicus the juror Falcula 'had sat not in the turn of his own decury, not according to the law',[158] and his complaint that on Verres' instigation Q. Curtius, a *iudex quaestionis*, had been making *subsortitiones* into his jury 'from this decury of yours, of which I ought to have the freest disposal', with the object of reducing the number of senators available for Cicero's own eventual *subsortitiones*. He clearly implies that Curtius' action is illegal, and says he has managed to stop it.[159] The system of *subsortitio* suffered from the grave defect that supplementary jurors might be enrolled when the trial was nearly over. They had the choice of voting on hearsay or of demanding a rehearing of the case (*ampliatio*), which would not have made them popular if it had been grinding on for several months already. The case of Falcula was, in fact, a great scandal: he was enrolled by *subsortitio* on the jury trying Oppianicus; he asked for no *ampliatio* but after three or four days gave what proved to be the casting vote for condemnation.[160]

After the *lex Aurelia* of 70 B.C., the juries, being drawn in equal numbers from the three decuries of senators, *equites* and *tribuni aerarii*, could be larger, and a larger allowance was no doubt made for rejections. A standard number for a jury seems to have been seventy-five. Cicero addresses the 50 *equites* (amongst whom, as often, he includes the *tribuni aerarii*) in the trial of Flaccus;[161] he speaks of awaiting the 75 votes in an imaginary trial of Piso;[162] in the trial of Scaurus 22 senators, 23 *equites* and 25 *tribuni aerarii* voted,[163] and in that of Gabinius there were 32 votes on one side and 38 on the other[164] (in both cases there were evidently a few abstentions). In another case, that of Procilius for parricide, only 22 and 28 votes are recorded;[165] the text may be corrupt, but it is equally possible that smaller juries were empanelled for murder cases than for political ones. In the trial of Clodius for sacrilege[166] fifty-six jurors voted; unless there was an unusually large number of abstentions this implies a jury of 57 or perhaps 63.

Under the *lex Pompeia de vi* an entirely different procedure was prescribed. All the 360 jurors on the special album were summoned and heard the evidence for three days; on the fourth day lots were prepared and on the day after that 81 names were drawn. These 81 on the same day heard speeches for and against the accused, two hours for the prosecution and three for the defence. Either party then rejected five jurors from each decury, and the remaining 51 voted.[167] It appears from the voting figures that the decuries were not equal, there being eighteen senators, seventeen *equites* and sixteen *tribuni aerarii.* The system would make bribery very difficult, but it must have been tedious for the 360 to listen to evidence for three days, knowing that for 309 of them it would be wasted labour.

On the day fixed for the trial, if the accusers having been duly summoned failed to appear the case was struck off the list, but they could re-initiate it at a later date from the beginning if they wished.[168] If the accused failed to appear he was forthwith condemned in absence.[169] A clause of the *lex Acilia* directs the praetor to carry on the trial if the accused '[...]rit aut in exilium abierit',[170] after the *nominis delatio* and before the judgment. Mommsen's restoration '[mortuus e]rit' is somewhat questionable: in the law of the Principate a criminal charge lapsed with the death of the accused unless he committed suicide to avoid condemnation (though it is true that exception was made in the case of *maiestas* and *repetundae*); and penal civil actions also normally lapsed if the accused died, though only before *litis contestatio*.[171] There seems to be only one Republican case in point, that of Licinius Macer, who was accused of extortion before Cicero. According to Valerius Maximus he committed suicide as the votes were being cast and sent a message to Cicero 'se non damnatum sed reum perisse, nec sua bona hastae posse subici', whereupon Cicero 'de eo nihil pronuntiavit'.[172] This would prove the point, were there not a different version in Plutarch, who makes Macer commit suicide after hearing of his condemnation—and it is this version which is borne out by what Cicero himself says of the matter.[173]

The order of proceedings enacted by the *lex Pompeia de vi*—

evidence first and speeches afterwards—was the reverse of the normal. According to Cicero, under the *lex Acilia* 'many persons were accused once, pleaded their case once, the witnesses were heard once, and they were condemned';[174] not that under the *lex Acilia* this always happened, for if after hearing the two speeches and the evidence more than a third of the jurors declared 'non liquet' there was an adjournment (*ampliatio*) and the whole case had apparently to be re-heard.[175] Glaucia introduced a compulsory adjournment (*comperendinatio*),[176] so that a trial henceforth consisted of an *actio prima* and an *actio secunda*, each consisting of the speech of the accuser or one or more of his *subscriptores*, the speech of the defendant or one or more of his *patroni*, and the hearing of evidence. There was not, it would appear, a repetition of the whole of the evidence given at the *actio prima*, but additional witnesses were brought forward to meet points that had arisen in the *actio prima*. This order of proceedings will explain why in some speeches (presumably delivered in the *prima actio*) Cicero alludes to the evidence as yet to come, while in others (presumably delivered in the *secunda actio*) he depreciates evidence already given.[177] In the *pro Flacco* he refers to his cross-examination of hostile witnesses in the *actio prima*, but also to a witness whom the accuser is going to call; and he announces his own intention of calling more witnesses to prove a particular point.[178] *Comperendinatio* is only expressly mentioned in connexion with trials for *repetundae*, and it so happens that references to evidence already heard occur only in speeches in the extortion court, the *pro Fonteio* and *pro Flacco*. But the evidence as a whole is so meagre that it would be rash to exclude the possibility that *comperendinatio* was under later legislation extended to other courts.

Witnesses could be cross-examined and subjected, like Vatinius in the trial of Caelius, to vituperative speeches designed to impugn their credibility. Much evidence was, however, provided in written form: this applied in particular to the evidence of cities, where a decree of the council—or council and people—often made under oath was presented by one or more delegates of the city.[179] It was usual also to bring in evidence to character (*laudationes*): Scaurus had nine consulars amongst his *laudatores* and most of them sent in their testimony *per tabellas* because they were away from Rome.[180] But ordinary private evidence was also accepted in written form. The witness had to take an oath and write out his testimony in the presence of sworn witnesses, who affixed their seals.[181] Written evidence could be read out in court in the course of the speeches, and so might have a more telling effect than spoken evidence given a day or two later.

Under the *lex Acilia*, after the speeches have been made and the evidence heard the jury holds a preliminary discussion to discover how many are prepared to vote for condemnation or acquittal. As we saw, if more than a third say 'non liquet' the praetor must adjourn the court and the whole case is reheard on another day, at the end of which another discussion is held. This could in theory go on *ad infinitum*; but the praetor may impose a fine of 10,000 sesterces on any juror who refuses more than twice to vote. When at least two thirds of the jury are prepared to vote the remaining jurors are removed and the willing ones vote by ballot. Each receives a ballot marked on one side 'A' (for *absolvo*) and on the other 'C' (for *condemno*). He rubs out one or the other, but there is nothing to prevent him rubbing out both. He then drops his ballot into an urn. When all the votes have been collected they are declared, those on which both 'A' and 'C' have been deleted being announced as 'sine suffragio', and counted. If the 'C's are in a majority the accused is declared guilty by the praetor; if there is a majority of 'A's or a tie he is declared not guilty. It is not stated whether the blank votes were taken into account in this count, but probably they were not: the 'non liquet' votes had already been eliminated, and the fact that the blank tablets were announced as 'no vote' implies that they were ignored.[182]

In the Ciceronian age the preliminary discussion had been abolished, and the final vote was carried out by the same procedure as under the *lex Acilia*, except that the blank votes now seem to have been treated as 'non liquet'. At the trial of Oppianicus thirty-two jurors voted, and of the votes some were 'non liquet' and only five were acquittals; yet if one condemnatory vote had been reversed Oppianicus would have been acquitted. It is not conceivable that a man would have been condemned on a vote of six 'condemno', five 'absolvo' and twenty-one 'non liquet': the 'non liquet' votes must have counted with the acquittals, and the voting will thus have been 17 'condemno', 5 'absolvo', and 10 'non liquet', so that the switch of one vote would have produced a tie. It appears from Cicero's language that the jurors who voted 'non liquet' were hoping thereby to secure a second trial. They did not want to acquit a guilty man, he says, nor, when they suspected that some of the jury had been bribed to condemn him, to vote for his condemnation straight away without investigating the suspicion: they would prefer to condemn him a little later when the matter had been cleared up.[183] It may be conjectured that if more than a third of the votes had been 'non liquet' the case would have been re-heard.

Cicero states that at the trial of Clodius for sacrilege fifty-six jurors voted, twenty-five for guilty and thirty-one otherwise, and that if four jurors had voted differently Clodius would have been condemned. Plutarch on the other hand says that the majority of the jurors handed in tablets with (both) letters deleted, to avoid committing themselves either way. This might imply that the jury was of the standard size of 75, and that nineteen voted 'non liquet' and their votes were not counted. But it may equally well mean that a considerable number of the votes that were not cast against Clodius were 'non liquet' votes.[184]

Under the *lex Cornelia* the defendant, or perhaps either party, could demand that the voting be open, the order of voting being determined by lot. Cicero speaks of this as being no longer the rule in 66 B.C., and it was no doubt abolished by the *lex Aurelia*.[185]

After the verdict has been given, the *lex Acilia* enjoins the praetor to put to the jury the question whether the accuser has been guilty of *praevaricatio*, deliberate failure to secure a condemnation.[186] The jury voted on this; their vote carried no direct penalty, but an accuser thus condemned became *infamis*, suffering various legal disabilities including incapacity to make another accusation. No provision is made in the *lex Acilia* for a condemnation for *calumnia*, malicious and unfounded accusation, but there were probably votes on both *praevaricatio* and *calumnia* under the judiciary laws of the late Republic.[187]

In most of the courts the pronouncement of sentence by the praetor ended the case, as the penalty was laid down in the relevant law and followed automatically upon conviction; neither the praetor nor the jury had any discretion.[188] What the penalties were under the various laws is often doubtful or unknown. It appears that in several laws the penalty was still under Sulla's legislation officially death, although in practice (and, in a sense, in law) a condemned man was allowed, if he could afford it, to go into exile in a foreign city and adopt its citizenship, thereby forfeiting his Roman citizenship; he was prevented from recovering it by returning to Italy, by a plebiscite forbidding him fire and water. In practice, then, the penalty was exile with loss of citizenship; in law it was death, and exile was not a penalty of the law.[189] Cicero was himself the first to introduce exile as a penalty in his *lex Tullia de ambitu*, but it was temporary exile only, for ten years, and did not carry loss of citizenship.[190] Clodius' law of 58 B.C. against persons who executed Roman citizens uncondemned seems to have been the first to enact prohibition of fire and water, *aquae et ignis interdictio*, as the formal penalty;[191] and the *leges Iuliae de maiestate* and *de vi*, passed in Julius Caesar's dictatorship, had the same feature.[192] This implies that the penalty for *maiestas* under the *lex Cornelia*, and under the *lex Appuleia*, must have been formally death.[193] The same is probably true of the *lex Cornelia de sicariis*; we have only the statements of the imperial jurists, who speak of the penalty as either *aquae et ignis interdictio* or *insulae deportatio* (the latter, of course, belongs to the Principate).[194] They give the penalty of the *lex Cornelia de falsis* in the same way.[195] That of the *lex Iulia peculatus*, which succeeded Sulla's law, is given as *aquae et ignis interdictio*.[196] The two Republican laws *de vi* were superseded by the *leges Iuliae de vi publica* and *privata*. The former is presumably the law of Julius Caesar which Cicero says enacted *aquae et ignis interdictio* as its penalty; the jurists give that or *deportatio*.[197] For *vis privata* they say that the penalty is confiscation of a third of the condemned man's property.[198] The penalties under the *lex Fabia de plagiariis* seem to have been pecuniary in the original statute.[199] Those of the various laws *de ambitu* are better known to us; they are somewhat peculiar. Persons convicted under the *lex Cornelia* were excluded from office and from the senate for ten years; the *lex Calpurnia* added a fine, and Cicero's *lex Tullia* imposed ten years' exile.[200]

For *repetundae* (about which we have much more information, though obscurities remain) there was not a fixed penalty in the same sense. The state enforced restitution: under the *lex Calpurnia* and the *lex Iunia* simple restitution was the rule; under the *lex Acilia* it became double,[201] and we know of no change under either of the *leges Serviliae*. It has been argued from the fact that Cicero in the *divinatio* against Verres announces a claim for 100 million sesterces against him and in the *actio prima* estimates his extortions at 40 million,[202] that Sulla must have raised the rate of damages from twice to two-and-a-half times; but it would be uncharacteristic of Roman legal practice to have made so niggling a change, and it is more likely that Cicero, before he had studied the evidence, made an exaggerated guess which he did not repeat when it came to the formal charge. When, then, the jury had voted and the praetor pronounced that the defendant was guilty in a given province of extortion of a global sum, it was then for the jury to make an assessment of damages (*litis aestimatio*), reviewing each claim in the light of the evidence already given, accepting or rejecting it and assessing the amount due under it. It was apparently possible at this stage to put in new claims which had no connexion with the case just tried but came under the statute of *repetundae*, and it was for the jury to admit or reject them.

Now such claims might presuppose offences under other statutes, which might be capital, and are in such cases styled *lites capitis* by Cicero. For example, one Septimius Scaevola was condemned on a charge of *repetundae* for offences committed in Apulia; but he had a claim lodged against him for accepting a bribe as juror to condemn Oppianicus for murder, an offence which came under the *lex Cornelia de sicariis*. The acceptance of that claim by the *repetundae* jury did not, of course, mean that the capital charge involved was legally proved, but it provided presumptive evidence for a prosecutor in the appropriate court. Cicero alleges that many people had been assessed for damages on charges which amounted to *maiestas* ('lites maiestatis', he calls them) and had subsequently been tried for *maiestas* on those charges and acquitted.[203]

That, however, is not the end of the matter. It appears from the *senatus consultum Calvisianum* that it was possible under Julius Caesar's *lex Iulia repetundarum* to bring a capital charge.[204] On the other hand, Caesar is said to have removed persons convicted under that law from the senate, and the *Digest* names among the penalties of the law that the condemned may not make a civil prosecution, give evidence, or be a judge.[205] From this it is necessary to conclude that there must have been two scales of penalty: money restitution (with *infamia*) for simple extortion; death for extortion aggravated by violence or judicial corruption.

Under the *lex Cornelia* there were certainly cases of the milder penalty: Cicero's remarks in the *pro Cluentio* about people who were condemned for extortion but subsequently acquitted of treason show this. Under the *lex Servilia Glauciae* Rutilius Rufus was condemned to huge damages and went voluntarily into exile.[206] But the severer penalty may also have existed under both these laws: Cicero's language in several passages of the *Verrines* implies as much of the *lex Cornelia*.[207] It is therefore possible that Glaucia, if it was he who made the *quaestio repetundarum* a full *iudicium publicum* in which any citizen might accuse, also introduced the death penalty.

Another thing that could be done at the *litis aestimatio*, under Glaucia's *lex Servilia* and later laws, was to claim money from any person to whom the condemned man was alleged to have passed on his ill-gotten gains, provided that evidence of such a transaction had been given at the trial. Cicero at any rate claimed that the trial of Rabirius Postumus on such a charge was irregular because no evidence had been given that he had received money from Gabinius;[208] and it was perhaps on this ground that Laterensis in 51 B.C. refused to admit such a charge against Servilius, made by Pausanias, for receiving money from Claudius Pulcher the proconsul of Asia.[209] Such subsidiary trials were heard by the same jury that had tried the principal case.

A clause of the *lex Acilia* prohibits all magistrates from obstructing trials,[210] and this rule must have become general, for we never hear of tribunes attempting to use their veto. (Vatinius, it is true, appealed to the tribunes when summoned for trial, but his was a *iudicium publicum* of the other type under the *lex Licinia Iunia*, not a regular standing *quaestio*.)[211] The same clause of the *lex Acilia* implies that the court did not sit on days when the senate or the *comitia* were convened; and in Cicero's day the courts were also suspended on holidays and during *ludi*, with the exception of trials for *vis*.[212] Another Acilian rule was that charges made after 1 September were to be differently handled from those made from 1 January to 1 September. The damages were apparently to be simple instead of double,[213] and it seems likely that this was because the case would not be tried before a jury but would go to *recuperatores*. Cicero speaks of leaving Rome in September, 'when the Forum has cooled off from trials', and returning in January.[214] There was then, it would seem, some kind of vacation in the last four months of the year. Cases already begun before 1 September went on, and the praetors and *iudices quaestionum* had to be in Rome,[215] but they did not initiate new trials except *extra ordinem*. Cases were given this status if the offence alleged was a particularly heinous one like parricide,[216] or a danger to the peace like some forms of *vis*,[217] or was closely linked with a case just concluded; thus Cluentius, having secured the condemnation of Scamander, the poisoner who had attempted his life, obtained priority for the trial of Fabricius, the agent involved in the attempt, and once again for the trial of Oppianicus, who was ultimately responsible.[218] The status *extra ordinem* meant in term that a case had priority over others on the list of the court concerned, and in vacation that it was given immediate trial instead of waiting until 1 January. Caelius' story about Sempronius Rufus, who accused his own accuser in order that the appearance of an 'extraordinarius reus' would hold up his own trial,[219] implies that any charge by any accuser of any defendant, if accepted *extra ordinem*, was sufficient to produce that effect. The explanation appears to be that the *extra ordinem* case would have absolute first claim to a jury, and no jurors were available except those engaged on Sempronius' case; presumably it was the only one dragging on in vacation, and the members of the album were not liable to serve in vacation unless they had already been empanelled before 1 September.

Accused persons were not normally arrested, even when charged with capital crimes, but were allowed to be at liberty not only up to but even after condemnation. Milo after his condemnation under the *lex Pompeia de vi* was tried and condemned in absence three further times on various charges, and did not leave Rome till a few days after this.[220] Caesar, as quoted by Sallust, asserted in 63 B.C. that a *lex Porcia* and other laws permitted exile to condemned people;[221] perhaps these laws gave them a period of grace to go into exile. We know of no person of the upper classes who was executed after condemnation on a capital charge by a *iudicium publicum*, but we often hear of exiles. Whether these advantages applied equally to humbler persons is more doubtful. When the assassin Avillius was dragged to the Columna Maenia and denounced Oppianicus as his employer to Manlius the *triumvir capitalis*, Manlius in turn dragged Oppianicus out of his house, but is severely criticised by Cicero for having taken no further steps; the implication is that he should have held him.[222] And Valerius Maximus tells a tale about a free-born woman, evidently of humble status, who was condemned to death and handed over to the triumvir for execution. The gaoler put off hanging her, and eventually she was reprieved by the praetor and his *consilium iudicum*.[223]

The courts were not very successful, either, in seizing the property of those condemned on capital charges or extracting full damages in cases of *repetundae*. The procedure laid down by the *lex Acilia* was that after sentence the praetor caused the condemned person to give sureties to the quaestor for an amount fixed by the jury, or, if adequate sureties were not given, caused his property to be sequestered and sold.[224] This made it easy for an accused, when he saw which way things were going, to convey his property to relatives and friends. Gabinius offered no sureties, and his property, when seized, proved insufficient to cover the damages.[225] At any rate, the exiles of whom we hear seem to have been comfortably off: Antonius, Cicero's colleague in the consulship, retired on condemnation (on an unknown charge) to Cephallenia; he owned the whole island and founded a city on it —or would have done if he had not been recalled before he had finished off the work.[226]

Roman statesmen, whatever their political views, seem to have been in agreement that the *iudicia publica* were an improvement on the *iudicia populi*. Bitterly though they might quarrel over the composition of the juries, *optimates* and *populares* alike created new jury courts, and thus reduced the role of the popular assembly in the administration of criminal justice. It was not until the dying days of the Republic that two political commentators expressed doubts about the system. The author of the *Epistula ad Caesarem* did not condemn the *iudicia publica* outright; he disapproved of the selection of jurors on a high property qualification and recommended larger juries drawn from the whole of the first class. Cicero in the *de legibus* was much more radical; there is not a trace of *iudicia publica* in his ideal republic, and criminal jurisdiction has gone back to the magistrates and assembly.[227]

In fact it is difficult to see that *iudicia publica* were superior to the old trials before the assembly. A jury of fifty or seventy-five was, it is true, better able to follow complicated evidence and assess its credibility than a crowd of thousands; but the praetor did not assist it by any summing-up, and it seems rarely to have decided on the evidence. Juries, to judge by the speeches delivered to them, were as vulnerable to irrelevant emotional appeals as any mass meeting. They were moreover strongly affected by political prejudice. In the court of *repetundae* the original senatorial jurors were notoriously lenient to their fellow-senators;[228] and after fifteen years of equestrian jurors Crassus could claim that senators were enslaved to the *equites* and beg the people to 'tear us free from the fangs of these whose cruelty cannot be slaked save with our blood'—rhetoric, of course, but not without basis.[229] In 92 B.C. an equestrian jury gave a notorious example of vindictiveness by condemning the scrupulously upright Rutilius Rufus for alleged extortion.[230] When the juries were restored to the senate the pendulum swung back, and Verres might well have been acquitted but for Cicero's vigilance and energy. After Aurelius Cotta's compromise political bias is naturally less evident, but Cicero's letters make it plain that any provincial governor who gave offence to the *publicani* stood in danger from the equestrian two-thirds majority on the juries.

Another defect of the *iudicia publica* was that in certain circumstances a man could be tried twice for the same offence, a weakness often exploited in political quarrels. The *lex Acilia*, it is true, enacted that no accusation should be made on a matter already judged under the law, whether the accused had been condemned or acquitted, and a further clause extended this ban to matters judged under the earlier Calpurnian and Junian laws.[231] The same rule was doubtless enacted in each of the laws constituting *iudicia publica*; but there were a number of offences which came under more than one law. The *lex Licinia de sodaliciis* dealt with organized electoral corruption, the successive laws *de ambitu* with all forms of electoral corruption; Milo was accused and condemned within a few days both *de sodaliciis* and *de ambitu* for the same offences. In the same way there were three *leges de vi* in force, the *lex Pompeia* which applied only to the disturbances of the year 52, and the *leges Lutatia* and *Plautia*, which dealt with various kinds of *vis*. Milo was condemned under the *lex Pompeia* and a few days later under one of the other laws, probably the *Lutatia*. His follower Saufeius was acquitted under the *lex Pompeia* and again accused, and again acquitted, under the *lex Plautia*. Judicial corruption came normally under the statute *de repetundis*, but if it led to a capital condemnation it also fell under that *de sicariis*, as in the case of Septimius Scaevola.[232] There was also an overlap between the *lex Cornelia de maiestate*, which dealt with such offences as leaving one's province or entering a kingdom or making war without the permission of the senate and people, and the *lex Iulia de repetundis*, which covered the same offences, presumably if undertaken in consideration of bribes.[233]

On the relative dilatoriness of *iudicia populi* and *iudicia publica* something was said in Chapter 1.[234] A *iudicium populi* might occupy only four actual days, though they would be spread out over a period—in the case of Clodius' prosecution of Milo from 2 February to 17 May.[235] Trials in the *quaestiones* were no better, with their postponements for *inquisitio* and their potential (and often actualized) opportunities to exploit procedural delays. But the gravest fault of the *iudicia publica* was corruption. It was said to have been rampant in the senatorial courts under the *lex Calpurnia*. According to Cicero, in the fifty (actually forty) years that the juries were equestrian not a breath of suspicion had touched them,[236] but this *ex parte* statement is not borne out by other evidence: according to Appian bribery gradually began after the death of C. Gracchus and was rife by the tribunate of Livius Drusus,[237] and this is confirmed by Drusus' attempt to establish a court for the trial of judicial corruption and the strenuous opposition offered to his proposal by the equestrian order.[238] From some of Cicero's speeches, especially the *Verrines* and *pro Cluentio*, it is evident that judicial bribery was commonplace, one might almost say regular, in his day. Judicial corruption was, of course, common in most cities of the ancient world unless stringent precautions were taken against it. The Athenians were fairly successful in stopping it, partly by empanelling very large juries and thus making it a hopelessly expensive operation, and partly by limiting trials to a single day, selecting the jury in the morning and making it vote the same evening, so that the parties had in any case no opportunity of getting at the jurors. Pompey in 52 B.C. tried both these devices in a modified form, as has been seen above,[239] but normally the Romans took no mechanical precautions against bribery, and jurors were for months accessible to agents of the parties. Their only idea was to choose their juries from the wealthiest classes, on the assumption—continually disproved in practice—that a rich man would not be tempted by a bribe. This belief was as strongly held by *populares* as by *optimates*: when they expelled senators they replaced them by the wealthiest class of non-senators; and a slightly less wealthy class was introduced by Aurelius Cotta but rejected again by the *popularis* Caesar.

The law on judicial corruption was scandalously inadequate. C. Gracchus had passed a law against judicial conspiracy to secure capital condemnations which, as was argued above, was probably directed against special courts set up by the senate under plebiscites, and therefore applied only to senators, who would sit on such courts.[240] It did not apply to pecuniary cases, such as those of the *quaestio repetundarum*, nor did it apply to bribery to secure an acquittal in a capital case. It was incorporated in Sulla's *lex de sicariis*, and was still available in Cicero's day against senatorial jurors who had accepted bribes to vote for condemnation in a capital case.[241] But the normal law under which judicial corruption in general was prosecuted in Cicero's day was the *lex repetundarum*.[242] The *lex Acilia* was clearly not intended to be used for this purpose; it was directed against provincial governors and their assistants, and its application was consequently limited to senators; and it could only be used even against senatorial jurors by a rather forced interpretation of the law, whereby the party that gave the bribe accused the juror who took it of having extorted it from him. A litigant who had bribed a jury, even unsuccessfully, would be unlikely thus to incriminate himself, and the law cannot have applied to judicial corruption until the right to accuse was thrown open to all citizens, by which time all jurors were *equites*. During the period of senatorial juries from 81 to 70 B.C. the *lex repetundarum* could indeed be used, but from 70 onwards it was only available against the senatorial third of the jury. The *equites*, having long enjoyed immunity from prosecution for bribery, came to regard it as an established privilege of their order,[243] and indignantly defended it against Livius Drusus in 91;[244] and a similar attempt by Cato in 61 was one of the principal causes of the breakdown of Cicero's 'concordia ordinum'. Cicero, speaking before mixed juries, goes out of his way to defend it, on the specious ground that since *equites* had voluntarily foregone the splendours of senatorial rank they should be freed from the risks and responsibilities of senators;[245] but in his letters he frankly admits that the equestrian case is a shabby one.[246]

The opening clause of the *lex Cornelia de sicariis* ordered that 'the praetor or *iudex quaestionis* to whom the court of murder shall be allotted, in so far as it occurs in the city of Rome or within one mile of it, shall investigate with the jury that has been allotted to him by law'.[247] A clause of the so-called *lex Iulia municipalis* excluded from the city councils of Italian towns anyone 'who has or shall have been condemned by a *iudicium publicum* in that municipality, colony, prefecture, *forum* or *conciliabulum* to which he belongs'.[248] It would seem to follow that the Roman courts had jurisdiction in Rome only, and that the Italian cities had their own criminal courts. This would not apply to the courts which dealt with political offences against the Roman people, such as *maiestas*, *repetundae*, *peculatus* or *ambitus* (though the cities may well have had their own procedures to deal with bribery in their local elections and embezzlement of civic funds),[249] but it would apply to murder, forgery, kidnapping and other 'ordinary' crimes. There is, unfortunately, no test case to prove or disprove this hypothesis. In the few trials of which we know, although all the persons concerned came from municipal towns —Ameria, Larinum, Tarracina—the alleged murder was either certainly committed or attempted in Rome or may have been so.[250] Milo was, it is true, tried at Rome for the murder of Clodius at Bovillae, but that was under a special statute enacted for trial of that particular offence.[251] Seeing, however, that the *lex Rubria* allows to municipal courts only a very limited jurisdiction in civil cases—only up to 15,000 sesterces in ordinary suits and only up to 10,000 sesterces and with the defendant's consent in suits involving *infamia*[252]—it seems very unlikely that municipal courts would have been allowed a criminal jurisdiction. The alternative is to hold that the *lex Cornelia de sicariis* set up two courts, one for offences in Rome and the other for offences in Italy; in fact we know that in 66 B.C. there were two courts *de sicariis* sitting as well as one *de veneficis*.[253]

As for the *iudicia publica* of the Italian cities referred to in the *lex Iulia municipalis*, they must be the courts frequently mentioned in municipal charters for trying offences against local bye-laws for which a fine was laid down. In the charter of Tarentum for one offence, embezzlement of municipal funds, the right of accusation is reserved for magistrates, while for another, demolition of a house, any citizen may accuse.[254] At Urso in the surviving clauses any citizen may accuse in all cases, but in one clause prescribing procedure it is envisaged that in some circumstances a magistrate will be the accuser and in others a private citizen.[255] An accuser applies to one of the *duoviri*, who serves summonses on up to twenty witnesses, residents of the city, appoints *reciperatores* by lot, the parties having a limited right of rejection, and fixes a day for the trial. Some trials had to be completed in a day; for the rest it was laid down that they must not begin earlier than the first hour nor continue after the eleventh. The principal accuser was allowed four hours and his *subscriptor* two, the defendant or his counsel twice as long. If the *reciperatores* failed to give judgment on the appointed day the *duovir* had to summon them and the defendant and appoint another day not more than twenty days later than the first. If an accuser failed to appear the accusation lapsed, though if he was a magistrate and was detained for reasonable cause the case could apparently be postponed.[256]

In the provinces all criminal trials we know of in the Republican age were, with one exception, tried by the governor sitting with a *consilium*. The one exception is the trial of a slave alleged to have violated a peculiarly holy sanctuary of Ceres at Catina; here the case was judged by the whole council of the city according to the laws of Catina.[257] The fact that the accused was a slave is probably not the relevant factor; local jurisdiction according to local law was probably allowed for religious reasons. All provincial criminal trials we hear of were also trials of peregrines.

The procedure was closely modelled on that at Rome. The governor did not initiate a case, but received charges from private accusers. When Verres wanted to get a criminal sentence against a Sicilian he had to put up an accuser: when Agathinus, whom he had expected to accuse Sthenius, refused to do so, he was at a loss until Pacilius stepped into the breach, and when Pacilius failed to turn up at the trial Verres did condemn Sthenius who was also absent; but this is represented by Cicero as the final *reductio ad absurdum* of the whole case: '. . . the man whom you condemned in absence not only without a charge and without a witness, but even without an accuser'.[258] It was apparently normal for the accused to be present when his name was received: this was the initial irregularity in the case of Sthenius. Verres might, according to Cicero, have claimed that it was legitimate for a name to be received in absence, for no law forbade this being done in a province. But in the senate many took a different view: 'whereas Sthenius has been charged in absence, that no judgment be passed on him in absence, and if it is passed, that it be not valid'. The tribunes of the plebs supported this view by exempting Sthenius, when he was condemned, from their edict forbidding persons condemned on capital charges from being in Rome.[259]

At the trial the governor sat with a *consilium*. The fullest account of a *consilium* is of that which was assembled for the trial of Philodamus of Lampsacus, who was accused of having killed Cornelius, Verres' lictor. Nero, the proconsul of Asia, was naturally the judge, but Dolabella, proconsul of Cilicia, whose legate Verres was, insisted on attending with all his staff. The *consilium* therefore consisted of Dolabella, his legate Verres, and doubtless his other legates and his quaestor and, Cicero says, his prefects and military tribunes; Nero's corresponding officers; and a number of resident Roman moneylenders, of whom one acted as accuser.[260] The governor was evidently bound by convention to invite the senior members of his staff to sit with him for important cases: Cicero condemns Verres for not summoning his quaestor and his legate for the trial of the captains of the Sicilian fleet but sitting only with his *comites*, his unofficial staff.[261] It was also evidently more or less obligatory to call in prominent members of the local Roman community: Verres called them in at Syracuse for the trial of Sopater although he knew that they had acquitted Sopater on the same charge under his predecessor.[262] It would seem, then, that although there was no legal obligation to assemble a *consilium* a *sententia sine consilio* was regarded as a travesty of justice, [263] and that though no law obliged a governor to call this or that person there was an accepted convention that the officers of his staff and local Romans of substance ought to be asked to sit on the bench. It would seem, moreover, that though the governor was not by law required to pronounce according to the voting of his *consilium* he was morally bound to do so. Cicero speaks of Philodamus of Lampsacus being 'condemned by a very few votes';[264] and the implications of what he says in the case of Sopater point the same way. Sopater's friends thought it impossible that the same men should condemn him on the same charge on which they had previously acquitted him, and Verres got over this difficulty not by overriding the votes of his *consilium* but by ordering one of them to go off and try a civil suit for which he had been appointed *iudex*, and permitting him to take with him a *consilium* of his own which included several more members of Verres' own *consilium*; others now begged to be excused, and Verres was left with the clerical members of his staff, on whose vote he proceeded to condemn Sopater.[265]

There is no recorded case of the trial of a Roman citizen in the provinces on a criminal charge during the Republican period. Gavius of Consa was summarily executed by Verres; but Verres professed not to believe his claim that he was a Roman citizen.[266] It may be presumed that the correct procedure, as in the case of Pleminius and his associates,[267] would have been for the governor to hold a trial, or at any rate an investigation, and if he thought the charge proved or provable to send the accused under guard to Rome to be tried in the appropriate *iudicium publicum*.

APPENDIX TO CHAPTER 2

THE DEFINITION OF *EQUITES* AS JURORS IN THE *IUDICIA PUBLICA*

The jurors whom C. Gracchus substituted for senators in the *quaestio repetundarum*, and who with some vicissitudes manned the courts down to Sulla, are called by Cicero and all later writers *equites*; so are the jurors of one of the three decuries brought into being by the *lex Aurelia* of 70 B.C., and so are those of the three decuries under Augustus. *Prima facie* it would be probable that the term *equites* bore the same meaning throughout the period, but it is of course possible that the definition changed.

The relevant clauses of the *lex Acilia* exclude senators and their near relatives and those who hold or have held offices which were the normal preliminaries to a senatorial career. The positive qualification is missing from both clauses. It is generally agreed that it cannot have been simply 'possession of a public horse' ('qui equum publicum habebit'), because—in Cicero's day, at any rate—the members of the eighteen centuries with the public horse were all very young men,[1] and under the *lex Acilia* jurors had to be at least thirty (the age was later raised to thirty-five).[2] It would also have been unnecessary in that case to spend words prohibiting the enrolment of senators, because they had been ordered by plebiscite a few years previously to return their public horses, and so no senator could be a member of the eighteen centuries.[3]

It has therefore been proposed that the qualification was 'present or former possession of a public horse' ('qui equum publicum habebunt habuerint'). This is a perfectly possible solution. A third alternative is that the qualification was expressed in terms of the equestrian *census* ('qui $\overline{\text{CCCC}}$ HS plusve census erit'). That there was a census qualification for equestrian status whether *equo publico* or *equo privato*, and that a list of those so qualified was maintained by the censors, is attested by Polybius.[4] The actual figure is first mentioned by Horace.[5] In favour of this last hypothesis a passage of Pliny the Elder has been adduced, in which he says that Gracchus first distinguished the equestrian order under the name of *iudices*, that after the civil wars they came to be known as *publicani*, and that Cicero established the title *equites* in his consulate.[6] The last part of the statement is certainly inaccurate, since Cicero was using the term *equites* for the pre-Sullan jurors as early as 70 B.C., and refers to a man with the *census equester* as an *eques* as early as 76.[7] Nor have we any evidence for the order being called *publicani* in the years after Sulla. It may, however, be true that members of what was later the equestrian order were, as Pliny states, called *iudices* in the period following the *lex Acilia*; and it has been argued that this would have been unlikely if they could have claimed, as present and past holders of the public horse, the full and honourable title of *equites*.

Under the *lex Aurelia* of Cotta the courts were shared between senators, *equites* and *tribuni aerarii*. The last class must derive its name from the *tribuni aerarii*, known only to the antiquaries Cato, Varro and Festus,[8] who had once been paymasters of the troops. They are spoken of in the past tense, and never mentioned in the Ciceronian period; they must have been, as a practical office, long obsolete in 70 B.C. It is hardly conceivable that a group of sinecure *tribuni aerarii* continued to be appointed every year, but it is conceivable that the censors still, by force of inertia, kept a list of persons qualified to serve, since a census qualification was probably required for a post with financial responsibilities. If so, the praetor Aurelius Cotta, looking for a suitable name to give his third group of jurors, may have revived the obsolete term which denoted a census class. Commenting on a passage of Cicero's speech against Clodius and Curio, the scholiast says:

> 'Tullius says that these jurors will not return the money they have received lest they should subsequently be unable to be in the number of the jurors under the Aurelian law, either because by returning the money they would be admitting they had been

corrupted or because, having lost 300,000 or 400,000 which they had accepted from the accused, they would relapse into poverty and therefore could not [be enrolled in the number] of the jurors'.[9]

The scholiast may be wrong, but he evidently conceives the qualification (or one of the qualifications) for jury service to be a property one, and the figures he gives for the bribes to be returned strongly suggest that it was 400,000 for an *eques* and 300,000 for a *tribunus aerarius*.

One of the changes which Pompey introduced in 55 B.C. was to select jurors of the highest census from the three decuries.[10] There is an argument that this implies that the basic qualification for membership of the decuries must have been something other than a census qualification. Such was, of course, certainly true any way of senators, and it could have been true of *equites* if possession of the public horse, past or present, was the qualification; but it is hard to see what other qualification than property the *tribuni aerarii* can have had. The whole argument is invalid in any case. *Equites*, on the census qualification theory, might own a bare 400,000 or a million or more, and Pompey directed that the richest be selected; *tribuni aerarii* had both an upper and a lower limit, but the praetor could perfectly well choose those nearer to 400,000 than to 300,000.

Julius Caesar abolished the decury of *tribuni aerarii*; Antony added a new third decury of centurions. Cicero protests in the *First Philippic*.[11] Centurions, he declares, have always been eligible for jury service under Caesar's recent law, under the *lex Pompeia* of 55 and under the *lex Aurelia*. Antony replies: 'but a census qualification was required'. There can hardly be a plainer implication that no qualification except property was required for jury service—except, naturally, in the senatorial decury. On the other hand Cicero's counter to Antony's reply is somewhat ambiguous: a property qualification, he says, was required not only for a centurion but also for a Roman Knight. He might mean that an *eques equo publico* did not automatically qualify as a juror unless he had the *census*; but he more probably (if slightly illogically) means that no one ranked as an *eques Romanus* without the *census*.

Under Augustus there were originally three *decuriae iudicum*.

In A.D. 4 he added a fourth, whose members were of a lower census (200,000 sesterces) and acted only as judges of minor civil cases. Gaius added a fifth, probably of the same kind.[12] The composition of the three principal decuries, which were distinguished as *selecti* and alone provided juries for the criminal courts, is obscure. Senators still served in the courts: the *curatores aquarum*, senators, were excused 'iudiciis privatis publicisque'; Augustus ordered that no courts be held on the days allotted to sessions of the senate; and the younger Pliny tells one of his correspondents about a senator who has been fined by the praetor of a *quaestio* for failing to appear for jury service.[13] There were even still *tribuni aerarii* among the jurors, according to the elder Pliny;[14] there is no confirmation at all of this, but it is possible that Augustus, who undid so many of his adoptive father's reforms in his zeal to restore the old Republic, did revive the *tribuni aerarii*. Augustus's decuries must, however, have been of uniform composition, since he allowed the decuries a year's vacation in rotation,[15] and it can hardly have been the case that one year the juries were half senators and half *equites* and the next half *equites* and half *tribuni aerarii*. They were, moreover, very large, each nearly a thousand strong,[16] so the senate could not have provided a full decury. It is probable therefore that each decury contained senators, *equites* and perhaps *tribuni aerarii*; but the bulk were *equites*: the *decuriae iudicum*, which was their official title, are in literary language sometimes called *decuriae equitum*,[17] and individual jurors occasionally describe themselves as *equites*.[18]

Now were these jurors *equites equo publico* or persons with the equestrian census? According to Pliny the Elder, when Augustus drew up the decuries the majority of the jurors wore the iron ring, the name *eques* being at that time confined to *equites equo publico*;[19] and according to Seneca a man could become a judge merely by *census* and *equestris hereditas*.[20] In inscriptions of the Principate some *iudices* of the decuries are described as *equo publico* but most are not: *I.L.S.* 6747, of the Augustan period, is a dedication to two men, probably brothers, of whom one is described as 'equo publico, iudici de IV decur.', and the other as 'iudici de IV decuriis equiti selectorum publicis privatisq.'; the latter was clearly not *equo publico* or he would have said so. Later inscriptions which record a 'iudex $\overline{\text{CCCC}}$ Romae decuriarum V', a 'iudex $\overline{\text{CCCC}}$ selectus' and a man 'ex quinq. decur. iudicum inter quadringenarios'[21] show that the *equites* who manned the three principal decuries were qualified by a census of 400,000 sesterces.

If the persons called *equites* were so qualified under Augustus, and, as Cicero implies, had been so qualified under the *lex Aurelia*, there seems little reason to doubt that the *iudices* of the *lex Acilia* were citizens owning 400,000 sesterces or more.

CHAPTER 3

THE CRIMINAL COURTS OF THE PRINCIPATE

THE *iudicia publica* continued to function during the early Principate. Augustus by the *lex Iulia de adulteriis coercendis* added another court to their number,[1] and also enacted a new statute for the court of electoral corruption, the *lex Iulia de ambitu*;[2] and either he or Julius Caesar passed a new law *de peculatu*.[3] The arrangements that were made for manning these courts, and the qualifications required for jury service, have already been described.[4]

Under Augustus there also appear three entirely new criminal courts at Rome, that of the emperor himself, that of the consuls presiding over the senate, which becomes a court of law as it had never before been, and that of the prefect of the city. The evidence for the senatorial court is unequivocal: in A.D. 22 Tiberius at the trial of Silanus, proconsul of Asia, caused to be read out to the senate the indictment of Volesus Messalla, proconsul of Asia in about A.D. 12, and the decree of the senate passed against him.[5] Tacitus also alludes to the banishment to Crete for defamation of Cassius Severus by the judgment of the senate under oath;[6] it was probably at about the same time. Ovid, speaking of his exile in A.D. 8, complains to Augustus:

nec mea decreto damnasti facta senatus
nec mea selecto iudice iussa fuga est;[7]

clearly at that date the senate was a normal court that could be spoken of on a par with the *iudicia publica*. On the other hand it is improbable that the senatorial court existed as early as 22 B.C., when Primus, Fannius Caepio and Varro Murena were tried for *maiestas* before the regular *quaestio*,[8] for it was just such cases that the senate later normally undertook. It has been argued that the *senatus consultum Calvisianum* of 4 B.C. implies that the senatorial court still did not exist at that date, since it lays down that 'if any of the allies after the passing of this *senatus consultum*, having been deprived of money publicly or privately, wish to seek restitution, provided they are not bringing a capital charge against the person who took it', they are to approach any magistrate who has the power of convening the senate, and he will in the presence of the senate appoint a small panel of judges from the senate.[9] This might indeed imply that capital charges had to go to the *quaestio repetundarum*, but the inference is not quite cast-iron, for the passage might equally imply that capital charges could not be made to any magistrates but the consuls themselves, who would arrange a full senatorial trial.

The evidence for the court of the emperor himself is much weaker, consisting mainly of anecdotes. Cassius Dio has a story that Maecenas, watching Augustus sitting in judgment and suspecting from his demeanour that he was about to impose death sentences, wrote a note, 'Rise now, executioner', and flung it into his lap.[10] In Suetonius there are three relevant stories.[11] He says that Augustus, trying a manifest case of parricide, endeavoured by leading questions to prevent the accused from confessing and so incurring the appalling penalty of the 'sack'. He also gives an account of Augustus trying a case of a forged will and, to prevent all the witnesses to the will from being punished according to the *lex Cornelia*, handing out to his assessors not only tablets of acquittal and condemnation but also a third, absolving witnesses who had signed in ignorance. In the third story the emperor is trying one Aemilius Aelianus from Corduba (the charge is not specified), and reprimands the accuser for trying to prejudice him by alleging that the defendant has spoken abusively of him. Finally Dio, under the year A.D. 10, has a more circumstantial account: a quaestor had been accused of murder, and prevailed on Germanicus to be his advocate. The accuser asked Augustus to take the case himself on the ground that Germanicus would exercise undue influence on the jurors of the regular *quaestio*; but the emperor refused.[12] These stories do not perhaps add up to anything very impressive; what is conclusive is the conduct of the emperor Tiberius at Piso's trial. One accuser, Fulcinius Trio, first lodged a charge with the consuls, but Tiberius was soon asked to take the case; he held a preliminary investigation and decided to send it back to the senate.[13] Tiberius clearly considered judging the case himself, and in view of his strict adherence to Augustan precedent this must imply that Augustus had exercised a capital jurisdiction.

The office of prefect of the city did not become permanent until the last years of Augustus. Tacitus, speaking of Piso, who was the first permanent prefect, says that it was his duty to discipline slaves and turbulent citizens;[14] what grew out of that we shall see later. The city prefect presumably derived his *imperium* from the emperor.

None of these courts was subject to *provocatio ad populum*, a fact which seems on the face of it to be in conflict with the *lex Iulia de vi publica* which had recently reaffirmed that right.[15] The suggestion has been made that the senate at first provided a show of legality for its actions by passing the *senatus consultum ultimum*. But the claim that a consul could execute citizens after the passage of an *S.C.U.* had always been strongly contested: Cicero had been exiled for doing so. And now the *lex Iulia* had reaffirmed *provocatio*. Nor do the sources give a hint of frequent *senatus consulta ultima*: they record one only, during the serious election riots of 19 B.C.[16] It seems utterly inconsistent with the ordered legality of the restored Republic to suppose that a state of emergency was frequently (still less permanently) declared merely to hold a trial. This explanation would, of course, also fail to account for the emperor's capital jurisdiction. It seems to be generally suggested that this developed gradually, from precedent to precedent; but there must be a first execution; there can be no gradual approach to that. And this explanation too is inconsistent with the meticulous legality of Augustus' approach to his constitutional position. There must have been legislation empowering the emperor and his delegates and the consuls to exercise capital jurisdiction without appeal. It may have taken the form of granting them *iudicii publici exercitio*. Papinian speaks of this as a special power, conferred by statute, *senatus consultum* or imperial constitution, to try cases arising under the *leges iudiciorum publicorum* such as adultery; and he states that it cannot be mandated like the ordinary jurisdiction inherent in a magistrate's *imperium*.[17] In point of fact all known trials before the senate and before the emperor are of *crimina iudiciorum publicorum*.

Both the emperor and the senate exercised *cognitio* and were therefore free from certain procedural rules governing the *iudicia publica*. They could accept and try together charges under two or more statutes:[18] in very many of the trials recorded under Tiberius *maiestas* was added to the principal charge.[19] They could also disregard the statutory penalties, not only reducing them but making them more severe[20]—even reintroducing the death penalty for offences, like *maiestas*, for which *aquae et ignis interdictio* had become the *poena legis*, as will be discussed below. Both courts were courts of voluntary jurisdiction. It was open to an accuser to present his charge either to the consuls or to the emperor. As we have seen, Tiberius after some hesitation refused to accept the charge against Piso;[21] so too the senate could refuse an accusation, usually referring it to the emperor.[22]

The senate normally tried political charges, such as *maiestas* and *repetundae*, against senators;[23] they sometimes took similar charges against *equites*.[24] They sometimes, but rarely, tried client kings.[25] They also can be found trying all kinds of criminal charges such as adultery, murder and forgery, brought against senators and women of senatorial rank.[26] Under the Flavians the senate developed the doctrine that it ought to have exclusive jurisdiction over the crimes of senators. Encouraged by Titus' declaration that he never had or would put a senator to death, the senate asked Domitian that the principle should be formally set out in a *senatus consultum*.[27] Domitian refused the request; but Nerva, Trajan, Hadrian and Marcus Aurelius are all stated to have taken an oath to this effect,[28] and Septimius Severus both took an oath and had a *senatus consultum* passed that senators should be subject to the jurisdiction not of the emperor but the senate.[29] Dio, in his recipe for an ideal principate put into the mouth of Maecenas, lays it down unequivocally that all capital charges against senators and their wives and children must be tried by the senate without any intervention by the emperor.[30]

Most emperors, including some like Hadrian and Severus who had taken the oath, did occasionally try senators on capital charges, especially *maiestas*, and it is very difficult to see on what principles, if any, they accepted or rejected capital charges presented to them. Tacitus implies that they normally tried their own freedmen and procurators,[31] and Pliny gives a concrete case: the heirs of Julius Tiro accused Sempronius Senecio, an *eques*, and Eurythmus, an imperial freedman and procurator, of forging some codicils to Tiro's will, but withdrew the charge out of respect for Eurythmus; Trajan insisted on their bringing it to clear his own good name.[32] On the other hand a procurator of Asia was tried before the senate for *repetundae* under Tiberius, and another, P. Celer, was possibly so tried under Nero.[33] Trajan took to himself a case of adultery between a centurion and a military tribune's wife, expressly emphasizing that he did so in the interests of military discipline;[34] yet under Nero a prefect of the Ravenna fleet came before the senate, apparently for *repetundae*.[35] And besides cases in which senators, procurators, imperial freedmen or military officers were tried there were many in which the defendant was undistinguished and not a member of the imperial administrative service or the army. Aemilianus Aelianus of Corduba, whom Augustus tried,[36] was apparently no more than a provincial worthy, as was Claudius Aristo whom Trajan tried;[37] and Pliny does not even mention the name of the widow who accused her deceased son's freedmen of forgery, and whose case was accepted by Trajan.[38] Cases came to the emperor's court not only from Rome and Italy but from all over the empire. They might be referred to him by provincial governors: thus, the adultery case of Gallitta, the military tribune's wife, was referred to Trajan by the consular legate, and Claudius Aristo must have been similarly referred by the proconsul of Asia. Cases also came up to the emperor on appeal from the provinces, first by *provocatio* and later by *appellatio*.[39]

The *iudicia publica* were not only exempt from *provocatio* but also protected against the veto of magistrates, and there was thus no possibility of appeal against them. Under the principate, however, their verdicts were not absolutely final. In 30 B.C. Augustus (as he was to be called) was given 'a vote of Minerva', that is a power of pardon, in all courts.[40] Tiberius, finding that Clutorius Priscus had been condemned by the senate for *maiestas* and straight away executed in his absence, procured a *senatus consultum* whereby condemnations in the senate should not be registered and executed until ten days had elapsed.[41] Later it would seem that all capital sentences were submitted to the emperor for his confirmation: we find Nero at the beginning of his reign declaring that he wished he could not write, when he was urged to subscribe 'in the usual way' to the punishment of a man who had been condemned to death.[42] A trial in the senate was subject to veto, and the emperors occasionally used their tribunician power to stop a trial.[43] It was also possible for an accused to appeal to the only magistrate who had a *par maiorve potestas* with the consuls, the emperor. One appeal to Tiberius is recorded by Tacitus and another to Nero.[44] The emperor Gaius regularly received appeals from the senate;[45] and Hadrian had to make a definite ruling that appeals should not be allowed to the emperor from the senate.[46]

The *iudicia publica* had a poor reputation in the early Principate. Tiberius made a practice of going into the courts and sitting on the bench beside the praetor; he did not interfere, but sometimes addressed the jurors on their duties in general terms, and thus (as Tacitus had to admit) prevented undue influence from being exercised on the court by powerful litigants.[47] By the reign of Nero the jurisdiction of the city prefect had evidently expanded so as to compete substantially with the *quaestiones*: in A.D. 61 a certain Valerius Ponticus was held to be guilty of *praevaricatio* for bringing charges against persons before the praetor (i.e. as a preliminary to a *iudicium publicum*) to prevent them being accused before the urban prefect and to secure their acquittal.[48] The political courts lost their business to the senate and the emperor, who seem to have taken over all *maiestas* and *repetundae* and perhaps *peculatus* too; and *ambitus* became rare when the elections were transferred to the senate and died out altogether when they came completely under imperial control.[49] By the time of the Severi, Paulus explicitly states that the *iudicia publica* have fallen into obsolescence.[50] It is impossible to determine when this came about. The equestrian *iudices decuriarum* continued to be appointed down to Commodus' reign (and there is one isolated example later, Petronius Volusianus who was consul in 261),[51] but this means little, for appointment as a *iudex* had long become an honorary distinction, frequently given to provincials or to men who pursued a procuratorial career, who could not have come to Rome to serve in the courts.[52] Even in Pliny's day casualness over attendance at jury service suggests that it cannot have been of much importance: he writes, it will be remembered, to a young friend who is an equestrian *iudex* to tell him that a zealous praetor of a *quaestio* has fined a senator, apparently for non-response to a summons; the praetor's action is, it seems, unprecedented, but now that the old order has been revived other praetors may take courage and follow the precedent.[53]

Apart from that taken by the senate and the emperor most of the jurisdiction formerly exercised by the *iudicia publica* went to the prefect of the city, who by the Severan period had jurisdiction over all crimes committed in Rome or within a hundred miles of the city.[54] But some criminal jurisdiction was also taken over by the consuls and praetors, who received *exercitio publici iudicii* by decree of the senate or imperial constitution, and exercised *cognitio* with a *consilium* of assessors. This is stated in rather obscure language by Dio in the speech of Maecenas; the urban magistrates are to judge all cases except murder and are to establish for this purpose courts of senators and *equites*. These courts are not juries, for the final decision is to rest with the magistrate, from whom appeal may lie to the city prefect.[55] Some support for this can be found in the legal sources: Ulpian cites a rescript of the emperor to the consuls on the law of adultery; and he had occasion in his book *de officio consulis* to discuss the duty of a judge to choose between several accusers.[56] These two passages might, it is true, refer to the consuls as presidents of a senatorial trial; more conclusive is Papinian's reference to a praetor trying a case of the murder of a master by his slaves: he is said to exercise his jurisdiction by decree of the senate and therefore not to have the right to mandate it to another.[57]

The *praefectus vigilum*, though not, in the eyes of Pomponius, a magistrate like the prefect of the city but an 'extraordinary appointment for the public benefit', had also by the Severan period acquired a minor capital jurisdiction, presumably mandated to him by the emperor: he dealt with arson, burglary, robbery and theft, though remitting particularly grave cases to the prefect of the city.[58] The *praefectus annonae* had a specialized jurisdiction over offences connected with the food supply of Rome.[59]

In Italy outside the hundred mile limit which was the border of the city prefect's jurisdiction, criminal jurisdiction was by the time of the Severi exercised by the praetorian prefects.[60] The question of the justification for the praetorian prefect's judicial functions, the reasons why he acquired them and the stages of their growth is exceedingly obscure. It might seem strange at first sight that the commander of the body-guard should become a judge; but judges were not expected to be legal experts and the prefect had the advantage of being very close to the emperor, *ex hypothesi* trustworthy, and perhaps with time on his hands. His judicial powers perhaps began with the delegation to him of individual cases: the case of the woman who accused her dead son's freedmen of forgery and murder was delegated by Trajan to Iulius Servianus,[61] who may have been praetorian prefect at the time. There is, too, a story of Marcius Turbo, prefect under Hadrian, already engaged in judicial business in the very early morning when others were just going home to bed.[62] Commodus is said to have delegated to his praetorian prefects a charge of treasonable divination brought against Septimius Severus.[63] But Ulpian provides the first definite evidence for a general delegation to the prefects of all cases of *plagium* committed in Italy beyond the hundred mile limit:[64] his discussion happens to be about *plagium*, but there is no need to infer that other cases did not come under the prefects' jurisdiction, though the rules varied for the different laws, as will appear. The praetorian prefects might also hear criminal cases from all over the empire, sent up to them on the emperor's orders. In the reign of Caracalla we hear of a Roman *eques* who had been relegated to an island being sent to Rome to be tried for murder by the praetorian prefects.[65] Severus Alexander gave a ruling that if the owners of goods stolen from a repository only required production of the *custodes* they could get that on application to the governor of the province; but if he thought the case more serious he was to remit it to Ulpian the praetorian prefect.[66] Part of a letter of Gordian III is quoted, saying: 'If Lysanias the decurion had given an undertaking to find the robber Barsagoras, he must either be made to produce him or be sent to the praetorian prefect or the provincial governor.'[67] Finally, according to Paulus, officials of the procurator who confiscate property without the authority of a judgment go for punishment to the praetorian prefects.[68]

The earliest evidence that we possess on the administration of criminal justice in the provinces under the Principate is contained in the edicts of Augustus to the province of Cyrene. They reveal that there were now jury courts like the *iudicia publica* at Rome, manned by resident Roman citizens aged over 25 and possessing property of at least 2,500 denarii. Delegations from Cyrene had convinced Augustus that there were frequent judicial conspiracies against the Greeks by the Romans, who collusively brought capital charges, gave evidence and voted. So to remedy this the emperor ordered that an equal number of Greeks should be enrolled on the album and that the property qualification for Greeks and Romans alike should be 7,500 denarii or at any rate not below half that sum. He ruled that if a Greek accused so opted the jury should consist of half Greeks and half Romans; the number was to be fifty, from which the accuser could reject two and the accused three.[69] Although Augustus is dealing with capital trials of Greeks, against whom the abuses had occurred, his language in the edict implies that Romans were tried in the same courts. 'If a Greek accused, being given the choice . . . ' implies that there could be Roman accused—and that they were given no choice; and the new panel of Greek jurors is established 'for the capital trial of Greeks'—not for Romans, who would still be tried by Roman judges. In another of the edicts Augustus speaks incidentally of capital cases 'in which the governor of the province must judge and decide himself or provide a court of jurors'.[70]

There is no other trace in the sources of such a system, but it is unlikely that it was peculiar to Cyrene, for which it was badly adapted, being clearly planned for provinces with a large and prosperous population of Roman citizens. It seems likely, therefore, that it was a general scheme applied to all provinces, even those least suited to it. The object may have been partly to provide a less arbitrary capital justice for provincials than the *cognitio* of the governor (though in that respect it failed signally in Cyrenaica), but it seems more likely that these courts were primarily designed for the trial of Roman citizens. Citizens were by now in some provinces very thick on the ground: there were in Narbonensis, Sicily, Tarraconensis, Baetica, Africa and Macedonia considerable numbers of *municipia* and *coloniae*, whole towns of Roman citizens. It must have been becoming increasingly difficult to cope with crime if every citizen charged with it could claim *provocatio* and demand to be sent to Rome for trial. It thus seems reasonable to believe that the *exercitio iudicii publici* which was given to the consuls and the emperor and his delegates was extended to proconsuls, and that jury courts were organized to conduct the trials. It seems unlikely that the governor of

Cyrenaica could arbitrarily choose between empanelling a jury and trying a case himself; he was probably bound to use the jury for crimes falling within the scope of the criminal statutes, *crimina iudiciorum publicorum*, but could exercise *cognitio* for *crimina extraordinaria*. In this latter case *provocatio* would still apply if the accused was a Roman citizen. These juries are never heard of again, and had certainly disappeared by the beginning of Trajan's reign: Marius Priscus, proconsul of Africa, could not have sold for a million sesterces the condemnation of two Roman *equites* and several of their friends, all executed save for one *eques* who was exiled, [71] if their cases had been tried by juries. It must be presumed that they fell into desuetude in the same way as the *iudicia publica* at Rome.

Exercitio iudicii publici was, naturally, normally given to provincial governors only; but there was in principle no reason why it should not be extended to others, and this was sometimes done in the case of particularly common crimes. Caracalla, for instance, gave capital jurisdiction under the *lex Fabia* on kidnapping and the *lex Iulia* on adultery to all procurators—not merely those who were provincial governors.[72] As there had been 3000 adultery cases awaiting trial in Rome a few years before,[73] there may well have been similar arrears in the provinces to justify the second of Caracalla's grants.

Notwithstanding the disappearance of jury courts in the provinces there is some evidence that provincial governors retained *exercitio iudicii publici*, in the sense that they could try statutory crimes without *provocatio*. Suetonius tells how Galba as governor of Spain in the latter part of Nero's reign condemned a Roman citizen to death for poisoning his ward, whose heir he was, and sentenced him to crucifixion. The man 'implored the laws' and testified that he was a Roman citizen, but Galba merely crucified him on a whitewashed cross higher than the rest.[74] The victim seems to have been complaining of the degrading penalty, normally reserved for slaves, rather than making a *provocatio*; and Suetonius regards the incident as evidence of undue severity in the repression of crime and not as a flagrant breach of the law. A second case in point is that of Flavius Archippus of Prusa.[75] He was condemned for forgery by Velius Paulus, proconsul of Bithynia, in or before A.D. 84, and sent to the mines. He later claimed to have been restored, and produced as evidence warm letters of Domitian recommending him to a later proconsul, Lappius Maximus (in or before 86) and making him a grant of land at Prusa. Archippus was clearly already a Roman citizen when he was tried, or he would have quoted the grant of citizenship as evidence for his restoration. He was evidently a favourite of Domitian, so that it would have paid him to appeal if that had been legally possible. In fact he never claimed that his condemnation was in any way illegal. Thirdly there is the case of Marius Priscus, which has already been described: it would obviously have been in the interest of the two *equites* and their friends to appeal, since they were being corruptly condemned. Priscus' behaviour shocked the senate as a monstrous piece of brutality and corruption, but there is no hint that they held condemning and executing Roman citizens without *provocatio* to be unconstitutional.

In two of these cases the charges were *crimina iudiciorum publicorum*, namely murder and forgery; the alleged offences of Marius Priscus' victims are not known. The condemned men seem in all the cases to have been of the upper classes: the Spaniard was apparently a man of property, Archippus was a philosopher, two of Priscus' victims were *equites*. Yet they were condemned and executed or sent to the mines and no *provocatio* was available to them. On the other hand citizens of very humble status indeed, accused of an *extraordinarium crimen*, Christianity, were sent to Rome for trial, or at any rate the emperor was consulted on their fate.

Among the powers voted to the future Augustus in 30 B.C. were an extended tribunician *auxilium*, the right to judge on appeal, and the 'vote of Minerva' in the *iudicia publica*, already mentioned.[76] The first and third of these powers are prerogatives of mercy in the field of criminal justice, so it seems likely that the second falls into the same category, and is not a power of appellate jurisdiction in civil cases but the right to judge instead of the people in cases of *provocatio*. Be that as it may, *provocatio ad populum* turned into *appellatio ad Caesarem*, and the two terms *provocatio* and *appellatio* became inextricably confused.[77]

The only account we possess of a *provocatio*, that of Paul before Festus, is unfortunately very confused, and one is led to suspect that neither Paul nor his biographer understood the legal position. Festus took his seat on his tribunal at Caesarea and summoned

Paul, with whom came the group of Jews who accused him of various breaches of the Jewish law. Festus asked Paul if he was willing to go to Jerusalem and be tried before him there. Paul appears to have been afraid that at Jerusalem Festus would come under undue influence from the Jews, and that he would be condemned and perhaps, despite an appeal, executed. He also, we know, was set on getting to Rome. He answered: 'I stand at the tribunal of Caesar, where I ought to be tried. . . . I appeal to Caesar.' Festus, after consulting his *consilium*, answered: 'You have appealed to Caesar: to Caesar you shall go'.[78] Festus had good reason to consult his *consilium*, for Paul's *provocatio* was irregular; he had not been condemned, and *provocatio* (and *appellatio*) could only be made after condemnation. But Festus was perhaps glad to send to Rome what looked like being a troublesome case, and so allowed the irregular appeal. He apparently regularized the position by deeming Paul to have been condemned: at any rate Paul went to Rome in chains under military escort.[79]

When Pliny was trying people accused of Christianity he executed peregrines forthwith if they obstinately refused to recant; but he sent Roman citizens in the same circumstances to Rome.[80] There is no hint here of appeal, and it is quite probable that zealous Christians courting martyrdom would not have appealed; it appears that provincial governors were under standing orders to remit to Rome citizens found guilty of *extra-ordinaria crimina*. At Lugdunum under Marcus Aurelius the governor, having arrested and tortured the leading Christians, condemned the recusants to be thrown to the wild beasts in the amphitheatre. He also rearrested those who had at the beginning of the persecution denied their faith and wrote to the emperor for a ruling on them. When the first group were thrown to the beasts the governor learnt that one of them, Attalus from Pergamum, was a Roman citizen, and immediately had him taken out of the arena and imprisoned with the second group to await the emperor's ruling. Those who had denied the faith were released on imperial instructions, but Attalus was again cast to the beasts.[81] Here we have a further development: Roman citizens need not be sent in person to the emperor, but his authorization must be obtained for their execution.

It must have begun to be felt anomalous that Roman citizens

found guilty of *crimina extraordinaria* were carefully protected, governors being obliged to send them to Rome or at least to consult the emperor before putting them to death, whereas citizens condemned for *crimina iudiciorum publicorum*, while tried in exactly the same way by the governor's *cognitio*, could be executed without appeal. *Appellatio*, appeal to the emperor as a *par maiorve potestas* of the governor, had been common since Augustus' reign in civil proceedings; it does not seem to have been applicable to criminal cases, where *provocatio*—originally appeal to the people, now to the emperor as representing the people—was the proper procedure except in so far as abolished by the grant of *exercitio publici iudicii* to the governor. Ultimately appeals were allowed in criminal cases: they are first mentioned in a speech of Marcus Aurelius, a rescript of the *Divi Fratres* and the writings of a contemporary jurist, Scaevola.[82]

Under the principate soldiers were no longer, as they had been—in theory, at any rate—under the Republic, protected by *provocatio*. According to Dio the privilege of 'wearing a sword' was accorded only to those magistrates who had the right of executing a soldier.[83] This must refer to the *ius gladii* mentioned in a few inscriptions and by the jurists. Dio says it should be granted to the consular legate of an army only, not to legionary legates or lower officers.[84] But it was also sometimes granted to equestrian governors, presumably presidial procurators who happened to have some Roman troops under them.[85] The inscriptions never mention it in connexion with *legati Augusti pro praetore*, presumably because for them it was routine: apart from the presidial procurators they record it for commanders of fleets or armies who are not provincial governors,[86] and once for a procurator of Moesia,[87] who perhaps had an emergency command. The earliest attested case of *ius gladii* is *I.L.S.* 9200, of the reign of Domitian; but mention of it is so rare that its origin may well be much earlier. At the beginning of Tiberius' reign Drusus executed two ringleaders of the mutinous Pannonian legions,[88] and a few years later Apronius the proconsul of Africa decimated a Roman cohort;[89] but most Roman commanders felt justified in taking drastic action in a crisis, whatever the law. It is perhaps more significant that Josephus describes Coponius, the first prefect of Judaea in A.D. 4, as having received from the emperor authority including that of life and death;[90] any governor, be he proconsul, legate or prefect, could execute peregrines, and this special power was hardly needed for resident Roman citizens in Judaea, who were very few, but it may have been needed for Roman troops such as the *cohors II Italica civium Romanorum voluntariorum*.[91]

W th the continued diffusion of Roman citizenship, particularly in certain provinces, the volume of *provocationes* must have become embarrassingly large. The problem was solved by the grant of special powers to some provincial governors. These powers are described in curiously vague language by the jurists. They sometimes speak of them as *ius gladii*,[92] but this is probably a solecism or looseness, against which Dio protests, emphasising that *ius gladii* applies only to soldiers. Sometimes they speak of a *merum* ('undiluted') *imperium*;[93] but more often of a power of *coercitio* or *animadversio*.[94] They all agree that such a grant is special, made by law, *senatus consultum* or imperial constitution, and the governor who receives it cannot mandate it to his legates as he can and normally does mandate the *imperium* inherent in his office. In the middle of the second century Venuleius Saturninus in his *de officio proconsulis* wrote: 'if there is anything that requires a greater punishment the legate ought to refer it to the proconsul. For he has not the right of punishing or chastising or flogging severely'.[95] It would seem then that in some provinces the new *merum imperium* was already granted under Pius or Marcus. In 203 at Carthage Hilarianus the procurator, who had received the *ius gladii* in place of the proconsul Minucius Timinianus, deceased, condemned and executed Vibia Perpetua, who from her name was presumably a Roman citizen, for Christianity.[96] The grant of Roman citizenship to all free inhabitants of the empire by the *constitutio Antoniniana* must have made the general grant of *merum imperium* to all provincial governors essential. We thus reach the situation envisaged by Dio: all provincial governors have capital jurisdiction over all civilians in their province; their legates and quaestors (and presumably the *legati legionum* and *iuridici* in imperial provinces) have no such jurisdiction. In addition those governors who command troops—who are all now Romans—have a *ius gladii* which empowers them to execute soldiers; their subordinate officers have no such power, but they are exempted from the *lex Iulia de vi publica* so that they can punish military offences, which probably means that they could flog soldiers and put them in irons, both forbidden by the clause of the *lex Iulia* that reaffirmed *provocatio*.[97]

Roman citizens had thus lost their ancient privilege of *provocatio*. In place of it they had *appellatio*. It was a less sure protection. Roman governors seem to have received very rigorous mandates about *provocatio* and to have sent the meanest citizen up to Rome automatically; the governor of Lugdunensis was so alarmed at having inadvertently thrown a Roman citizen to the beasts that he had him removed from the very amphitheatre. On appeals, on the other hand, the governor had a certain discretion, which was guided by imperial constitutions. He was authorized to execute forthwith, after condemnation, notorious brigands and leaders of civil commotion,[98] and he could also refuse appeals which he considered to have been made merely in order to delay execution, when the prisoner's guilt was manifest.[99]

Meanwhile the position of peregrines had perhaps improved somewhat; it is possible that when criminal appeal to the emperor for citizens came in it was also allowed to peregrines. We cannot be certain about this, because the legal sources as we have them have been purged of all references to peregrines, who no longer existed in Justinian's day. The evidence we do have is about decurions, and it is ambiguous whether decurions mean councillors of Roman (and no doubt Latin) cities or whether the word is used more generally to cover those of Greek and other foreign cities as well. Hadrian ruled that decurions should not undergo the death penalty except for parricide; they were subject to the penalty of the *lex Cornelia*, which was by now deemed to be *deportatio in insulam*.[100] This ruling was extended by Marcus Aurelius and Verus, who laid down that the maximum penalty for decurions for all crimes should be *deportatio*.[101] Now as a provincial governor was not authorized to deport, and—apart from the prefect of the city—only the emperor could assign a condemned man to an island, this meant that decurions had in effect an automatic appeal. The governor held the trial and condemned the defendant: he was then held while the emperor was consulted; the emperor might quash the verdict or assign an island.[102] Since there is no direct evidence whether peregrine decurions were covered by these rules it may be worth while to take some general considerations into account. The imperial government seems to have been genuinely concerned with the welfare of the provincials and in checking the brutality and corruption of governors. It might therefore have allowed appeal to peregrines on the same basis as to citizens. And secondly Dio considered it a matter of importance that the emperor should bind the provincial aristocracy to himself by protecting it against maltreatment by governors: the provincial notables would thus be loyal to him and check rebellions.[103] On this basis the emperors had fully as much reason to give judicial privileges to peregrine city councillors, who were often influential locally, as to those of Roman and Latin cities.

No more criminal statutes were passed after the *lex Iulia de adulteriis coercendis*; the scope of the criminal law was nevertheless considerably extended. This was partly effected by bringing new offences within the existing penal laws. The senate, or rather the majority of the senate, in Trajan's day held that they had the right to relax the law or to make it more severe,[104] but this seems to have applied to individual cases only. At the trial of Junius Bassus, for example, who admitted having received presents from the provincials, one party held that he must be condemned because the law forbade presents, but the majority felt that that by itself would not be a ground for condemnation, since it was a normal social custom;[105] the latter view was confirmed by later emperors.[106] The senate did, however, sometimes make substantive amendments to the law by *senatus consultum*. They ruled, for example, that castration came under the *lex Cornelia de sicariis*;[107] and although the law covered only those who made, sold, bought, kept or gave poison with intent to kill they brought under it those who sold love-potions and the like which proved fatal and paint makers who used without due care the numerous poisonous substances of their trade. And going even further than this they ruled that people whose armed slaves with their knowledge seized a neighbour's farm, and people who incited riots or failed to report shipwrecks, came under the *lex Cornelia*.[108]

The expansion of the law of *maiestas* seems to have been principally by interpretation and precedent. The crime under the statute is broadly defined by Cicero as: 'to derogate from the dignity, splendour or power of the people or those to whom the people has given power.'[109] Acts of treason against the state had been fairly fully defined in the Julian and earlier laws,[110] but we hear very little about offences against magistrates: this half of the law was exploited under the Principate by accusers who brought under it any trivial action which might be construed as reflecting on the dignity of the emperor. The rulings in the *Digest* that to repair decayed statues of the emperor or hit a statue of the emperor accidentally when throwing a stone do not constitute *maiestas* are a sufficient indication of the extremes to which this process was carried,[111] and Tacitus provides numerous instances of far-fetched charges.[112] He tells us also that it was Augustus who extended *maiestas* to cover libel, his motive being to inflict a severe penalty on Cassius Severus, who had published scandalous allegations about a number of men and women of high rank;[113] the extension from deeds to words, which shocked Tacitus, seems reasonable within the terms of the law: presumably, though Tacitus implies the contrary, only libels against magistrates, including the emperor, can have come within the law of *maiestas* (and it is curious, incidentally, that the *Digest* has nothing on this branch of *maiestas*).

There were some other extensions of the old statutes. Claudius, for instance, issued an edict that 'if any person, when writing another's will or codicils, writes in in his own hand a legacy to himself, he shall be liable as if he had committed an offence against the Cornelian Law', and a number of *senatus consulta* elaborated this provision;[114] and the use of false weights and measures was brought under this same statute by Hadrian.[115]

Much more significant, however, was the creation of entirely new *crimina extraordinaria* which had no connexion with the statutes. These crimes arose from the *cognitio extra ordinem* of the emperors, the city prefect, the praetorian prefect and the provincial governors. It had always been normal for provincial governors under the Republic to announce by edict that they would punish any one who followed a certain course of action, and such an edict would often be repeated by their successors and so become part of the 'provincial edict'. Thus after the great slave revolt M'. Aquillius and successive governors of Sicily made it a capital offence for a slave to possess a weapon.[116] Under the Principate also the initiative must sometimes have come from the provincial governors. In Egypt it was a capital offence to damage an irrigation dyke or to cut down mulberry trees (which were planted on the dykes to strengthen them); and in Arabia it was capital to place stones on a man's land (it was a warning that anyone who cultivated the land would be murdered).[117] These offences must have been created by the prefect of Egypt and the legate of Arabia respectively.

Other crimes were of general application, and it is more difficult to infer who took the initiative in creating them. Many were civil delicts coming to be treated as crimes: thus, for example, a victim could still sue a thief in the civil courts and get double damages; but it was more usual to accuse the thief criminally, whereupon he would receive appropriate punishment.[118] Some categories of thieves, those for instance who plied their trade by night or in the public baths, were apparently always treated criminally;[119] so also were cattle rustlers (*abigei*) and those who harboured brigands (*receptatores*).[120] Other new offences included various kinds of *iniuria*, from abortion, breaking up of marriages, abusive language and libel to soliciting of women, girls and boys; making a corner in wheat; violation of tombs; moving of boundary stones; fortune telling; the propagation of new religions; the profession of Christianity.[121] A criminal version of the civil delict of *dolus* was created, strangely called *stellionatus*;[122] and a gap in the civil law was filled by the *crimen expilatae hereditatis*: no civil action had been possible against a person who seized an estate before the heir took possession, because the estate was held to be ownerless at such a moment. Under the new law any citizen could bring a charge. This crime is first mentioned in a speech of Marcus Aurelius, and may have been invented by him.[123]

All judges trying cases *extra ordinem* had complete discretion as to penalties, within any limits that might be laid down by imperial mandates or rescripts. The variety of penalties available was greatly increased. First, besides the plain death penalty (decapitation with the sword) there were more unpleasant forms of death, such as crucifixion or impalement, burning alive or being thrown to the wild beasts.[124] Immediately below execution ranked hard labour in the mines; the sentence might be for a term of years or for life, and in the latter case it carried with it loss of liberty. The convicted man became *servus poenae*—with the curious result that a slave so sentenced, if pardoned, became a free man instead of reverting to his former owner.[125] Besides the mines there was also hard labour on public works, which was usually imposed for a term of years only and did not carry loss of liberty.[126] Next comes deportation to an island, which developed out of *aquae et ignis interdictio*.[127] Under the Republic a condemned man had been able to choose for his place of exile any free city which would accept him into its citizenship; but Augustus in A.D. 12 forbade exiles to reside on the mainland or any island within fifty miles of the coast except Cos, Rhodes, Lesbos and Sardinia.[128] We next find Tiberius and the senate assigning particular specific islands to exiles.[129] Deportation meant not only enforced residence on a remote island but loss of citizenship, though not of freedom. It could only be imposed by the emperor or the prefect of the city.[130] Relegation was different: an order either to reside within a given area, or more commonly outside certain named areas—normally one's own province and Italy. This sentence was generally for a term of years only, and carried no loss of status.[131] Finally came some minor penalties: expulsion from a city council or exclusion from civic offices;[132] prohibition from pleading in the courts or taking part in legal affairs;[133] flogging, beating or fines.[134]

All these penalties were applied not only according to the gravity of the offences but also according to the status of the offenders, divided broadly into two groups, *honestiores* and *humiliores*. The two terms are never defined by the jurists, and much was no doubt left to the discretion of the judge in borderline cases; but decurions clearly came above the line, and soldiers and veterans shared some of their privileges. By the end of the second century, it would seem, the penalties enumerated above had been divided into two groups, one appropriate to *honestiores*, the other to *humiliores*. The former might occasionally suffer the 'plain' death penalty, but normally *deportatio in insulam* was the worst they need fear, followed by *relegatio* and expulsion from the *ordo* or the bar. *Humiliores* were liable to the exacerbated forms of the death penalty, to the mines and public works, and to flogging and beating.[135] This class distinction in criminal penalties does not seem to have existed in the first century A.D. As we have already seen, Galba as legate of Spain under Nero condemned a citizen who was evidently a man of property to crucifixion, and under Domitian Flavius Archippus, who surely as a philosopher would have ranked as *honestior*, was sent to the mines; and one of Marius Priscus' victims in 97–8, an *eques Romanus*, suffered the same penalty.[136] The first extant evidence of the distinction is the rule of Hadrian, already quoted,[137] that decurions are to be exempted from the death penalty for murder (except in cases of parricide), and to be subject to the penalty of the law, now held to be *deportatio*. In another rescript of Hadrian it is laid down that upper-class people who remove boundary stones are to be relegated for a term of years, whereas their humble agents should receive corporal punishment and two years' hard labour on public works.[138] Antoninus Pius drew a distinction between a humble man who killed his adulterous wife and an upper-class one: the former was to be condemned to hard labour for life, the latter to be relegated to an island for a term of years.[139] Marcus and Verus exempted decurions altogether from the death penalty, making *insulae deportatio* the severest sentence that could be imposed on them.[140]

It was remarked in the previous chapter that under the Republic exiles seem to have got away with much of their property. Julius Caesar during his dictatorship, observing (we are told) that the rich were the more prone to crime because of this, confiscated the entire estates of parricides and half the property of other criminals.[141] Augustus in A.D. 12 ruled that exiles were not to retain more than 125,000 denarii[142] (but it is worth noting that this, 500,000 sesterces, was more than the equestrian census). In the senatorial trials under Tiberius each case seems to be treated on its merits and no general principle emerges: the property is sometimes confiscated, sometimes assigned to the accuser, sometimes to the heir, more usually divided between these claimants.[143] By the time of the Severan lawyers it is established law that all who have incurred the penalty of death or loss of citizenship or liberty suffer confiscation of their property; children are, however, entitled to a portion of their father's goods.[144]

The procedure of the *iudicia publica* in Rome remained, as far as we know, the same as under the Republic until they came to an end, and that of the new *iudicia publica* in the provinces seems to have been similar.

The senate as a court of law evolved a procedure in which the old rules of senatorial debate were blended with those of the public courts. A trial was set in motion by a *postulatio* followed by a *nominis delatio* to the consuls by an accuser (now often called a *delator*) supported by *subscriptores*.[145] The consuls summoned the senate. If, as was often the case, several charges under different statutes were included in an accusation, the house had to decide whether to hear them together or separately.[146] If there were no further complications the *delator* and his *subscriptores* and the defendant's counsel—and if he wished the defendant himself—spoke in the order prescribed in the *quaestiones*, speeches being limited in time by the water-clock; and after that, as in the *quaestiones*, evidence was heard.[147] Finally there was a debate and vote on verdict and sentence, conducted under the traditional senatorial procedure, the consuls asking the senior senator for his opinion and the others assenting to this or making other proposals. From the accounts of trials in Tacitus and Pliny it would appear that verdict and sentence were considered together.[148] Tacitus makes Tiberius say in an early trial for *maiestas* that he will vote openly and under oath to compel others to do the same,[149] which would seem to imply that the votes were normally taken unsworn and by ballot; but though the oath is mentioned in only one other passage, where it is said that Cassius Severus was exiled to Crete by a vote of the sworn senate,[150] it is difficult to believe that senators, unlike the people in the assembly and the jurors of the *iudicia publica*, took no oath; and in all records of trials the voting appears to be open: with the procedure followed it is hard to see how it could have been otherwise. Debate often followed on the disposal of the condemned man's property and on the rewards to be given to accusers or, in case of an acquittal, the penalties to be inflicted on them.[151]

In the case of trials for extortion the procedure was more complicated. There might be a capital trial, as above, or under the *senatus consultum Calvisianum*, as we have seen, if the provincials did not wish to bring a capital charge, they could approach any magistrate with authority to convene the senate, and he would introduce them into the senate, assign them a senator as advocate, and on the same day choose by lot four consulars, three praetorians and two other senators; out of these nine the two parties in the next two days alternately rejected four, and the remaining five within thirty days decided and assessed the claims. The plaintiffs were allowed to summon witnesses, but only from Italy and up to a maximum of ten.[152] By Pliny's day certain changes had taken place. It was now the senate which decided whether a capital trial should be held or the simplified 'civil' procedure used, and there might be debate between the accusers wishing to bring a capital charge and the defendant who wanted a 'civil' trial. Proceedings opened with the allocation of senators to be counsel for the accusers,[153] who were normally—but not always—delegates of the provincial *concilium*;[154] there was, however, nothing to prevent the latter from speaking for themselves.[155] We hear of one case in which the accused was assigned counsel by the senate,[156] but this must have been a special case. The next step was for the accusers to ask the senate for time—which might be as much as a year—and authority for an *inquisitio*, the collection of evidence and summoning of witnesses in the province.[157] This might lead to a debate, since the refusal of *inquisitio* might make a capital charge impossible. In one case the accused asked for permission to summon witnesses in his own defence, and this was ultimately, after a prolonged debate, granted by the senate.[158]

Alternatively the issue of capital or 'civil' proceedings might be raised directly by the accused, and this again could give rise to a debate. In the only case whose proceedings are recorded in detail Marius Priscus, former proconsul of Africa, pleaded guilty to simple extortion and asked for judges to be appointed to assess the damages, but Pliny and Tacitus, counsel for the Africans, objected on the ground that there were serious charges of judicial corruption against Priscus for which the 'civil' procedure was inadequate. After considerable debate a curious motion was adopted, that judges should be appointed for Priscus but that the witnesses to the alleged judicial corruption should be summoned. They were summoned, and a full capital trial followed which took three days; the senate sentenced Priscus to be exiled from Italy and the bribes he had taken to be confiscated.[159] In another trial Julius Bassus, who admitted having received presents from the provincials, was tried capitally although no more serious charges could be proved against him. As we have seen, the senators were in two minds: some thought that he must be found guilty and therefore expelled from the senate, as presents were forbidden by the law, others that simple restitution was enough, without loss of his rank. The latter sentiment prevailed, and judges were appointed to assess the value of the presents.[160]

In one case very briefly reported by Tacitus, which seems quite anomalous, the senate appears to have appointed a panel of judges to try charges that had nothing to do with *repetundae*.

Plautius Silvanus, praetor in A.D. 24, murdered his wife; and the emperor, having satisfied himself that a case for murder lay, referred the matter to the senate. The senate then, according to Tacitus, 'gave judges'. We know no more, for Silvanus committed suicide.[161]

The courts of the emperor, his great prefects, and provincial governors, whether proconsuls, legates or procurators, were of similar structure to one another and followed a similar procedure in capital cases. The magistrate sat, according to ancient custom, with a *consilium* of assessors. The emperor's *consilium* consisted mainly of senators: Claudius is represented as sitting with sixteen consulars and twenty other senators at the trial of Isidore of Alexandria (the author of the *Acta*, who seeks to magnify the importance of the case, no doubt exaggerates the rank and size of the *consilium*).[162] There was evidently no standing *consilium*, but senators were called to sit as occasion required: Pliny records at length one occasion when he was called to Centumcellae for three days and heard three cases, and alludes to two other occasions when he served.[163] In the second century it would seem that it became customary to summon the praetorian prefects and the 'principes officiorum' (the heads of the departments *ab epistulis*, *a libellis* and *a cognitionibus*).[164] Salaried members of the *consilium* also appear: they are very junior, being paid at the lowest scale of the procuratorial service and rising from this post to higher equestrian preferment: one describes himself as a lawyer ('iurisperitus').[165] As for provincial governors, Helvius Agrippa, proconsul of Sardinia in A.D. 69, records his *consilium* in full (this is in a dispute between two cities, but the composition of the *consilium* did not vary with the type of case): it consisted of his legate, his quaestor, and six others headed by his son, who were presumably his *comites*, or perhaps included some Roman residents of standing.[166] A second century proconsul of Africa was less exclusive: his list begins with six persons whose qualifications are not stated but who presumably include members of his senatorial and equestrian staff, and ends with four of his clerical staff, his *scriba quaestorius*, his *haruspex*, and two *scribae librarii*.[167]

When exercising *cognitio* a magistrate (including, of course, the emperor) took a much more active part in the trial than had the president of a *iudicium publicum*. This was inevitable when the accused had been denounced by a police official (an irenarch) or some other public official or by a private informer, so that there was no 'accuser'. In the case of Christians thus denounced Pliny interrogated the suspects, and if they denied that they were Christians he made them prove their denial by sacrificing to the gods and cursing Christ; but he took exactly the same line with suspects who had been properly accused, and did not leave the conduct of the case to the accusers.[168] Judges also cross-questioned witnesses.[169] In the *Acta Isidori* Claudius is found interrogating Isidorus and Lampon (who are at this stage the accusers) and in the *Acta Pauli* and the *Acta Appiani* Hadrian and Commodus are represented as holding dialogues with the parties.[170]

Under the rules of the old *leges iudiciorum publicorum* accusers were allowed to summon compulsorily—with the governor's consent—a limited number of witnesses, even from a distance. In the Principate the government sought to reduce the numbers so summoned and to discourage long journeys.[171] The *lex Iulia iudiciorum publicorum* laid down a list, which the jurists of the *Digest* adhere to, of people who could not be compelled to give evidence: relatives by blood or marriage of the accused and freedmen or patrons of himself and his family.[172] It also laid down the categories of persons disqualified from giving evidence: freedmen of the accused, minors, persons condemned in a *iudicium publicum* or in prison awaiting trial, those who have fought with wild beasts or prostituted themselves or been convicted of taking money for giving or withholding evidence.[173]

Several emperors gave instructions to provincial governors on how to evaluate evidence, and the jurists summarize their advice. Judges were to attach great weight to the rank and wealth of the witness, and to his general character and repute; but they were also to observe his demeanour in court, and to take account of whether all the witnesses on one side told the same premeditated story or could give consistent extempore replies under cross-examination.[174] Hadrian, indeed, attached such importance to the behaviour of witnesses under cross-examination that he refused to accept written *testimonia* such as had been freely admitted in the Republican courts, and sent letters to this effect to his governors.[175]

Slaves were examined under torture,[176] which alone was supposed to extract the truth from such lowly persons; though some emperors do seem to have known that torture was not infallible, since some people would say anything to bring it to an end while others were invincibly stubborn.[177] Slaves were tortured not only as witnesses but also as defendants, to induce them to confess or incriminate themselves.[178] They could not, however, be tortured (and therefore could not give evidence at all) against their owners, or their owners' guardians or mothers if they were minors,[179] except in cases of adultery, where they were normally the only possible witnesses,[180] and of *maiestas*.[181] Augustus invented a device for getting round the *lex Iulia* in the case of *maiestas*, which was borrowed by his successors, namely to have the slaves of the accused conveyed to the state;[182] and the same device was employed in the case of adultery.[183]

It was probably in the second half of the second century that torture was legally extended from slaves to free persons of low degree. Down to Antoninus Pius inclusive all references to torture in imperial constitutions, if they specify to whom they apply at all, specify slaves—except that Pius ruled that a *deportatus* could not be tortured,[184] and as a *deportatus*, though no longer a citizen, was still a free man, that might perhaps imply that peregrines were already in general liable to torture. Under Marcus and Verus there begin references to what look like free persons,[185] and Diocletian quotes a curious ruling by Marcus that the descendants of *eminentissimi* (praetorian prefects) and *perfectissimi* (other equestrian prefects and superior procurators) are to be free from 'the penalties and tortures of plebeians' down to the third generation;[186] it was presumably to protect such of them as might have sunk to the status of *humiliores*, but it implies that by the end of Marcus' reign, at least, torture of *humiliores* was standard. Most of the rescripts under Marcus, Severus and Caracalla still refer to slaves, but the Severan jurists speak explicitly of the torture of free persons, including freedmen (mostly discussing in what circumstances they cannot be tortured),[187] and Ulpian—again quoted by Diocletian—says that decurions and their sons are exempt,[188] which implies the contrary for *humiliores*. Diocletian ruled (and it was probably a reaffirmation) that soldiers and veterans and their sons were exempt.[189] But of course in practice for *maiestas* free persons, not necessarily humble, had sometimes been put to the torture notwithstanding the law,[190] ever since the time of Tiberius; and *maiestas* always remained an exception to any rules exempting the upper classes.[191]

Judges were always prone to think that torture was a short cut to the truth and to start torturing witnesses and the accused straight away; this became all the more common when torture was made applicable to free persons. Emperors frequently warned governors against this tendency, telling them not to start by torturing witnesses but to try to establish a case by argument, and in particular not to torture an accused unless there was a *prima facie* case against him.[192]

The imperial mandates to provincial governors contained the clause: 'the man in charge of a province must see to it that he clears the province of criminals'. Ulpian expands this: 'it is the duty of a good and conscientious governor to see that the province he rules is peaceful and tranquil, and this result he will achieve without difficulty if he takes careful measures to ensure that the province is free from criminals and searches them out. He should search out persons guilty of sacrilege, brigands, kidnappers and thieves and punish them according to their offences; he should also repress those who harbour them, without whom a brigand cannot long be concealed.'[193] As many governors had very few troops or none, and the government disapproved of soldiers being seconded to police duties, the hunting of brigands was left to the cities, who—in the eastern part of the empire—elected suitable persons from amongst whom the governor nominated irenarchs; they were provided with a force of mounted constables ('diogmitae').[194] When he had succeeded in catching a brigand the irenarch sent him up under guard to the governor with an *elogium*, which was apparently a brief report on the case. Many governors apparently executed brigands out of hand, but Hadrian and later emperors insisted that they must receive a proper trial: the irenarch (who was expected to have interrogated his prisoners as to their accomplices and harbourers) must be summoned and substantiate his case, and be commended if he proved it, reprimanded if he failed, and punished if he had falsified the evidence against the accused.[195] The governor's officials also might report criminals by what was called a *notoria*;[196] it was in such cases that a trial would be conducted without a formal *inscriptio* by an accuser (though even then the informer must appear to sustain his accusation).

Apart from the above cases the detection of crime and the bringing of its perpetrators to justice was still left to private citizens, either injured parties or personal enemies of the accused or else *delatores* for the sake of the financial reward. Pliny in dealing with the Christians in Bithynia accepted an anonymous letter denouncing a large number of suspects and acted upon it, arresting them and interrogating them himself; for this he was severely reproved by the emperor.[197] The proper procedure was for a private citizen to ask the governor for leave to accuse. Just as under the Republic, certain classes of people were wholly or partially debarred from bringing accusations: those condemned in a *iudicium publicum* (which came to mean condemned for one of the *crimina iudiciorum publicorum*) or convicted of *praevaricatio* or *calumnia* or bribery in a *iudicium publicum* (with the same extension); those who pursued various occupations deemed infamous, such as gladiatiors, actors and procurers; soldiers; women and minors, except for the murder of a near relative or testamentary forgery affecting themselves or near relatives; slaves, except for *maiestas*, for which any accuser was admissible; freedmen against their patrons.[198] On receipt of the application the governor fixed a period within which the accuser must make the formal *inscriptio*: we hear of a lady named Titia who was non-suited for failing to prefer her *inscriptio* in time.[199] If other accusers came forward meanwhile the governor decided which of them should conduct the case, giving due consideration to their status, age, character and interest in the case.[200] In making an *inscriptio* the accuser had to give an undertaking that he would persevere in his accusation until sentence was given, and furnish a surety for this.[201]

It was presumably at this stage, if not at the original *postulatio*, that the accuser served a copy of the charges on the accused,[202] and that the governor decided whether to imprison the accused, put him under military guard at his own house, or allow him to give bail or remain at liberty under his own recognizances. Here the governor had to consider the nature of the alleged crime and the status, property and character of the accused. According to Antoninus Pius an accused person prepared to give bail was not to be imprisoned except on very serious charges.[203] Those committed to prison might apparently wait some time for trial; governors were instructed to hold a gaol clearance at intervals, to which they were to invite local senators and barristers. The governor would discharge those prisoners who appeared to him on a cursory examination to be innocent, and reserve the rest for a proper trial;[204] there was, however, nothing to prevent him condemning a man on the spot if he thought his guilt manifest, and he was accordingly instructed to give due notice of a gaol clearance so that prisoners could prepare their cases and not be taken by surprise by their accusers.[205] A proconsul could delegate the task of gaol clearing to his legate, but in the case of Roman citizens the legate was entitled only to hold a preliminary investigation, and must send up all the prisoners to the proconsul,[206] who would normally no doubt release the ones found not guilty by his legate and try the rest. Imprisonment might be in various cities of the province, not necessarily the provincial capital; governors are warned to keep an eye on the local magistrates, who were liable to release prisoners without authorisation.[207]

If an accused—one, presumably, who had given bail or been allowed to stay at liberty, or who had evaded arrest—failed to appear to defend himself, he was not condemned in absence. The governor posted him as wanted, announcing this by edict and informing the magistrates of his town by letter, and his property was sequestrated. If he appeared within a year and stood his trial, and was acquitted, he recovered his property; if he did not appear the property was confiscated, and that was all the penalty he suffered.[208] Conversely, if the accuser failed to appear the case did not lapse forthwith. The accuser was summoned by edict, and it was only if he contumaciously ignored the summons that the governor, having summarily investigated the case, might acquit the defendant.[209] The accuser would, in such a case, become liable under the *senatus consultum Turpilianum*, which penalized all accusers who, having initiated a criminal charge, dropped it at any stage without obtaining a formal *abolitio* of the case by the magistrate.[210] If an accuser died while his case was pending or in progress it lapsed; but another accuser could come forward within thirty days.[211] If the defendant died the case was at an end 'unless the charge was one that continues against the heirs, such as *maiestas*; and the same is true of an accusation of *repetundae*, for that also is not ended by death'.[212]

Having condemned and sentenced the accused, or acquitted him, the magistrate then considered whether the accuser was guilty of *calumnia*, malicious prosecution, or *praevaricatio*, collusion to secure an acquittal, and if so punished him accordingly.[213]

NOTES TO CHAPTER 1

[1] See the references in Strachan-Davidson, *Problems of the Roman Criminal Law*, vol. I, at p. 131.

[2] Kunkel, *Untersuchungen zur Entwicklung des römischen Kriminalverfahrens in vorsullanischer Zeit*, passim, and *An Introduction to Roman Legal and Constitutional History*, pp. 61–2.

[3] Cic. *de legibus* III, 9.

[4] Ib. III, 6.

[5] Ib. III, 10.

[6] Ib. III, 9, 10, 11, 18, 33, 46.

[7] Ib. III, 8.

[8] Ib. III, 6.

[9] Ib. III, 10, 11.

[10] Ib. III, 27.

[11] Sallust, *Ep. ad Caesarem* II, 7, 11–12.

[12] Cic. *de leg.* III, 36; Auct. ad Herenn. I, 25, IV, 34; Cic. *de inv.* II, 72–3; Orosius V, 15, 24; cf. Cic. *pro Balbo* 28.

[13] Asconius, p. 80 (Clark); Cic. *div. in Caec.* 67.

[14] Asconius, p. 21.

[15] Auct. ad Herenn. I, 24; Livy, *Per.* 67; Licinianus, p. 13 Flemisch.

[16] Livy, *Per.* 69; Appian, B.C. I, 31; Cic. *de domo* 82.

[17] Cic. *pro Flacco* 77.

[18] Cic. *pro Rabirio perd. reo* 24; Val. Max. VIII, i, damn. 2. Decianus was himself condemned, and so was another tribune, Titius (Cic. loc. cit. and Val. Max. VIII, i, damn. 2, 3), but it is not clear whether these were popular trials.

[19] Appian, B.C. I, 33; Cassius Dio, frag. 95, 3 (Boissevain vol. I, p. 338).

[20] Cic. *Brutus* 179; Plutarch, *Sulla*, 10, 4; Cic. *pro Rosc. Amerino* 33; Val. Max. IX, xi, 2; Appian, B.C. I, 74; Vell. Pat. II 24, 2.

[21] Plut. *Lucullus* 37, 1–2.

[22] On the trials of Rabirius, see the Appendix to this chapter.

[23] Suetonius, *divus Iulius* 23.

[24] See below, p. 13

[25] Cic. *pro Sestio* 95; *in Vatinium* 40–1; *pro Milone* 40; Asconius, p. 48.

[26] Cic. *ad Quintum fratrem* II, 3, 1–2; 5, 4.

[27] Cassius Dio XLIV, 10.

[28] Cic. *I in Verr.* 36; *II in Verr.* v, 173.

[29] Cic. *de har. resp.* 7.

[30] Orosius V, 16, 8.

[31] For Pompeius' quaestorship see Broughton, *Magistrates of the Roman Republic*, I, pp. 560, 562.

[32] Val. Max. VI, i, 8.

[33] For the careers of the two Metelli Celeres see Broughton, op. cit., II, pp. 26, 41, 138, 141.

[34] Cic. *de domo* 45.

[35] Livy XXXVII, 57, 12.

[36] Id. XLIII, 16, 9.

[37] Asconius, p. 21.

[38] Livy XXV, 3, 13.

[39] Id. XXXVII, 58, 1.

[40] Id. XLIII, 8, 9.

[41] Id. XXV, 4, 8.

[42] *Schol. Bob.* p. 90 (Stangl).

[43] Livy XLIII, 16, 12.

[44] Aulus Gellius, *N.A.* VI, 9, 9 (=Valerius Antias fr. 60 Peter).

[45] Livy XXVI, 3, 9.

[46] Id. XLIII, 16, 11.

[47] Id. II, 52, 5; Dion. Hal. IX, 27, 3.

[48] Livy XXVI, 3, 5–9.

[49] See the Appendix.

[50] See note 26 above.

[51] Cic. *in Vatinium* 40.

[52] *Accusare* is normal, but *anquirere* perhaps more technical (Livy II, 52, 5; VI, 20, 12; VIII, 33, 17; XXVI, 3, 5–7). *Anquisitio* occurs only in Varro, *L.L.* VI, 90, 92.

[53] Cic. *pro Rabirio perd. reo* 6.

[54] Cn. Fulvius and P. Scipio and Claudius the censor spoke for themselves (Livy XXVI, 3, 1–4; XXXVIII, 51, 7–11; XLIII, 16, 14). Cicero and Hortensius spoke for Rabirius (Cic. *pro Rabirio perd. reo* 18) and Pompey and Marcellus for Milo (see note 26 above).

[55] Livy XXV, 3, 16; XXVI, 3, 5; XXXVII, 57, 13; Cic. *in Vatinium* 40; also in the mythical period Livy II, 52, 8; III, 13, 1–3 and 24, 3.

[56] Livy XXVI, 3, 7; XXXVII, 58, 1.

[57] Livy XXXVIII, 50, 5–52, 4.

[58] Appian, B.C. I, 74.

[59] Livy XXV, 3, 14–16.

[60] Id. XLIII, 16, 14.

[61] Aulus Gellius, *N.A.* VI, 19, 5 (from Nepos' *Exempla*).

[62] Suet. *div. Iul.* 12 'ac sorte iudex in reum ductus tam cupide condemnavit ut ad populum provocanti nihil aeque ad iudicis acerbitas profuerit'; Cassius Dio XXXVII, 26–7.

[63] Livy I, 26.

[64] Cic. *pro Rab. perd. reo* 15.

[65] Festus, p. 462–4 (Lindsay).

[66] Livy XXXVII, 51, 1–5.

[67] Id. XL, 42, 8–10.

[68] Cic. *Phil.* XI, 18.

[69] Trial of Horatius, Livy I, 26; of Rabirius, Cic. *pro Rab. perd. reo* 12; Suet. *div. Iul.* 12.

[70] Cic. *de re publica* II, 61; *de legibus* III, 11 and 44; *pro Sestio* 65.

[71] *Schol. Bob.* p. 90 (Stangl); Livy XLIII, 16, 14; Cassius Dio XXXVII, 26–7 (see Appendix). Tribes are specified in Val. Max. VIII, i, Absol. 7; Pliny, *N.H.* XVIII, 41–3, etc.

[72] Varro, *L.L.* VI, 90.

[73] Livy XXVI, 3, 9; XLIII, 16, 11; Aulus Gellius, *N.A.* VI, 9, 9.

[74] See note 72 above.

[75] See note 28 above.

[76] Cic. *de har. resp.* 7.

[77] Cic. *de legibus* III, 35–7; *Brutus* 97 and 106; *pro Sestio* 103; *de amicitia* 41; Asconius, p. 78.

[78] See Cic. *de legibus*, above.

79 *Schol. Bob.* p. 90 (Stangl); Livy XXIV, 43, 3; XXV, 3, 15; XXVI, 3, 7–8; XXXVIII, 52, 9–11 are cases of tribunes against tribunes. In the mythical period there is Livy III, 24, 7 (cf. 29, 6), tribunes against quaestors. Tribunes against aedile: Aulus Gellius, *N.A.* IV, 14, 6.

80 Cicero only boasts 'de perduellionis iudicio quod a me sublatum esse criminari soles', *pro Rab. perd. reo* 10.

81 Livy XXIV, 43, 2–3; Suet. *div. Iul.* 23, 1.

82 Livy XXV, 3, 15–17.

83 Aulus Gellius, *N.A.* VI, 19, 7.

84 Livy XXXVIII, 52, 9–11.

85 E.g. *Schol. Bob.* p. 90 (Stangl).

86 Livy XXXVII, 58, 1; XLIII, 16, 16.

87 *Schol. Bob.* p. 90 (Stangl).

88 Livy XXV, 4, 8 and 10–11; the mythical prototype is Quinctius Kaeso, Livy III, 13, 6–10. The case of Pleminius is exceptional, see p. 20.

89 Varro, *L.L.* VI, 90.

90 Livy XXXVIII, 52, 9–11.

91 Livy XXV, 4, 9.

92 Polybius VI, 14, 7–8; Livy XXVI, 3, 12; Cic. *de domo* 82; Appian, B.C. I, 31. Mythical examples of exile: Livy III, 13, 9; 29, 6; 58, 10; V, 32, 8–9; 43, 6; Cic. *de domo* 86. The legal principles of *exilium* are set out by Cicero in *de domo* 78; *pro Caecina* 100; *pro Balbo* 28. See further p. 77 below.

93 Val. Max. IV, vii, 3; VI, ix, 13; cf. Cic. *pro Balbo* 28.

94 Livy V, 32, 8–9.

95 Aulus Gellius, *N.A.* VI, 19, 8.

96 Id. III, 3, 15; Val. Max. VI, i, 10; Pliny, *N.H.* XXI, 8–9.

97 Val. Max. V, iv, 7.

98 Cic. *de legibus* III, 10.

99 The only historical case is that of Rabirius, for which see the Appendix.

100 See p. 10 with notes 65–8 above.

101 Varro, *L.L.*, VI, 90 and Orosius V, 16, 8.

102 Livy, *Per.* 19; Aulus Gellius, *N.A.* X, 6.

103 Aulus Gellius, *N.A.* IV, 14.

104 See note 28 above.

105 See notes 25–6 and 76 above.

106 Val. Max. VI, i, 7; Plutarch, *Marcellus*, 2.

107 See p. 6 with note 33 above.

108 Pliny, *N.H.* XVIII, 41–3 (=Piso, *Annales* fr. 33 Peter); cf. Broughton, *Magistrates* I, p. 353.

109 Livy XXXV, 41, 9–10; XXXVIII, 35, 5. In neither case is trial before the people specified, but analogous cases show that they must have been held.

110 Livy XLIII, 16.

111 Livy XXXVIII, 51, 1–4 (=Valerius Antias fr. 45 Peter); Aulus Gellius, *N.A.* IV, 18; Polybius XXIII, 14, 2.

112 *Schol. Bob.* p. 90 (Stangl); Val. Max. VIII, i, absol. 4; Cic. *de div.* II, 71; *de nat. deorum* II, 7.

113 Appian, *Hisp.* 83; Asconius, p. 80.

114 Livy XXVI, 2, 7–3, 12.

115 Auct. ad Herenn. I, 25; IV, 34.

116 Livy XXXIX, 40, 12; Val. Max. VIII, i, absol. 2; Diodorus XXXIII, 2; Livy, *Per.* 67; Auct. ad Herenn. I, 24; Licinianus, p. 13 F.

117 Livy XXII, 35, 3 (cf. 40, 3; 49, 11); XXVII, 34, 3 ff.; XXIX, 37, 9–10; XXXVII, 57, 12; XXXVIII, 51, 1; Aulus Gellius, *N.A.* VI, 19, 1–6 (there is a rival version—by Antias—in Livy XXXVIII, 54–5 in which L. Scipio was tried before a special court appointed under a plebiscite).

118 Livy XXIX, 16, 4–22; XLIII, 7, 8–85. 10.

119 Asconius, p. 21.

120 Val. Max. VIII, i, damn. 5–6.

121 Livy XXIV, 43, 2–3; XXIX, 37, 17, Val. Max. VII, ii, 6; Plut. *Cato maior* 19, 2–3; Aulus Gellius, *N.A.* III, 4 (cf. II, 20, 6; IV, 17, 1; VI, 11, 9).

[122] Livy XXV, 3, 8–5 (Postumius); XLIII, 16 (C. Claudius and Ti. Sempronius).

[123] Cic. *de domo* 82; Velleius II, 7, 3; Livy, *Per.* 61; Cic. *de oratore* II, 132; *pro Rab. perd. reo*, passim.

[124] Appian, B.C. I 31 and 33; Cassius Dio, frag. 95, 3.

[125] Cassius Dio, XLIV, 10, 1.

[126] Diodorus XXIV, 12.

[127] *Digest* 48.4.3.

[128] Livy XXVI, 2, 7–3, 9. Numerous institutions of the civil law, of course, existed *moribus* and did not derive from the Twelve Tables or subsequent statutes, such as *patria potestas* (*Dig.* 1.6.8 pr.), the prohibited degrees (*Dig.* 23.2.8 and 39), and the prohibition of gifts between husband and wife (*Dig.* 24.1.1).

[129] *Lex Osca tabulae Bantinae*, *F.I.R.A.* I, no. 16.

[130] The meaning of the word indicated by x is unfortunately quite obscure; neither of the usual translations, *caput* and *fundus liber*, can be justified.

[131] Livy III, 20, 7.

[132] Id. XXIX, 6–9; 16, 4–22.

[133] Id. XXVI, 15–16; 33–4.

[134] Polybius I, 7; Livy, *Per.* 15; Dion. Hal. XX, 5 and 16; Appian, *Samn.* 9, 2; Diodorus XXII, 1; Cassius Dio fr. 40, 7–12 (Boissevain, vol. I, pp. 119–20); Val. Max. II, vii, 15 fin.

[135] Livy XXVIII, 29, 9–12; Polybius XI, 30.

[136] Cic. *de re publica* II, 54.

[137] Livy X, 9, 4; cf. Cic. *pro Rab. perd. reo* 12–13.

[138] Sall. *Cat.* 51, 21–4.

[139] Cic. *pro Rab. perd. reo* 8. Further vague allusions to a Porcian law: Cic. *II in Verrem* v, 163; Sall. *in Ciceronem* 5 fin.; Asconius, p. 78.

[140] Aulus Gellius, *N.A.* XIII, 25, 12 (=Malcovati, *O.R.F.*^{2}, Cato, frag. 59).

[141] Hill, *Historical Roman Coins*, no. 36 (on pp. 66–7 and pl. X).

[142] Val. Max. IX, v, 1.

[143] *F.I.R.A.* I, no. 7, ll. 78–9.

[144] Plutarch, *C. Gracchus*, 9.

[145] Aulus Gellius, *N.A.* XIII, 25, 12 (see n. 140 above) and X, 3, 3.

[146] Sall. *Jugurtha*, 69, 4; Appian, *Numid.* 2; Plut. *Marius* 8.

[147] Polybius VI, 37. There are several later allusions to the *fustuarium* (Sall. *Hist.* IV, fr. 22 Maurenbrecher, p. 168; Velleius II, 78, 3; Cic. *Phil.* III, 14; Tac. *Ann.* III, 21) and two to the axe, both in revolutionary situations, Fimbria in 75 (*De vir. illust.* 70, 4) and Caesar in 49 (Frontinus, *Strat.* IV, 5, 2). The *fustuarium* is mentioned for early times, probably anachronistically, in 403 in a speech (Livy V, 6, 14), and in 471, in which case Livy II, 59, 10–11 specifies the axe for officers whilst the men are decimated; Frontinus, *Strat.* IV, 1, 34 just gives decimation for the mass; and Dionysius of Halicarnassus, IX, 50 says that the officers were executed with the axe and the soldiers with the *fustis*. This story suggests that when the annalist from whom it derives wrote both the axe and the *fustis* were, or had been recently, in use simultaneously. Perhaps the *fustuarium* was introduced as a punishment for other ranks, especially if large numbers had to be executed, as in a decimation, before execution by the axe came to be forbidden by law.

[148] Livy, *Per.* 57.,

[149] Cic. *de har. resp.* 7.

[150] Livy XLIII, 16, 12.

[151] Kunkel, *Untersuchungen*, pp. 71 ff.

[152] Livy, *Per.* 11; Festus, s.v. *sacramentum*, p. 468 Lindsay.

[153] Val. Max. VIII, i, damn. 5 and 6; Varro, *L.L.* V, 81; Asconius, p. 37; Livy XXXIX, 14, 10.

[154] Plaut. *Aulul.* III, ii, 2 (l. 416); *Asin.* I, ii, 5 (l. 131); Cic. *div. in Caec.* 50; *pro Cluentio* 39.

[155] Cic. *de legibus* III, 6; *Digest* 1.2.2.30; Sall. *Cat.* 55; Val. Max. V, iv, 7; VI, i, 10; VIII, iv, 2; Aulus Gellius, *N.A.* III, 3, 15; Pliny, *N.H.* XXI, 8.

[156] Festus, see note 152 above.

[157] Cic. *Brutus* 117; *Orator* 156.

[158] Livy XXXIX, 14–18; *F.I.R.A.* I, no. 30.

[159] Livy XXXIX, 41, 5–7; XL, 19, 9–10; 37, 4; 43, 2–3; 44, 6.
[160] Id. XLV, 16, 4.
[161] Polybius VI, 13, 4.
[162] Cic. *de finibus* II, 54.
[163] See pp. 20–21 above
[164] Livy XXXVIII, 54–5.
[165] Livy XLII, 21–2.
[166] See note 162 above.
[167] Cic. *Brutus* 85–8.
[168] Val. Max. IV, vii, 1; Cic. *de amicitia* 37.
[169] Orosius V, 12, 10.
[170] Livy, *Per.* 11 and X, 46, 16; Dion. Hal. XVII–XVIII, 4–5; Cassius Dio, frag. 36, 32 (Boissevain I, p. 109).
[171] Val. Max. VI, i, 11; Dion. Hal. XVI, 4 and 5; Livy VIII, 28.
[172] Livy X, 13, 14; 23, 11–13; 47, 4.
[173] Livy X, 31, 9. A temple of Venus.
[174] Val. Max. VIII, i, absol. 7, Livy VIII, 22, 2–4.
[175] Livy VII, 28, 9.
[176] Id. VII, 16, 9; Val. Max. VIII, vi, 3.
[177] Livy VII, 4; Cic. *de officiis* III, 112; Val Max. V, iv, 3; VI, ix, 1; Appian, *Samn.* 2; *de vir. illust.* 28.
[178] Livy VI, 19–20, esp. 20, 10–12.
[179] Id. VI, 1, 6.
[180] Id. V, 32, 8–9; Pliny, *N.H.* XXXIV, 13; Cic. *de domo* 86.
[181] Livy V, 29, 6.
[182] Livy IV, 40, 4 ff.; 41, 10–11; 44, 6–10; V, 11, 4 ff.
[183] Id. IV, 21, 3–4; Cic. *de domo* 86.
[184] Livy III, 56–8. Nor is the story (III, 33, 9–10) of the virtuous *decemvir* who held a murder trial before the people of great historical value.
[185] Livy IX, 26, 5–20; Diod. XIX, 76.
[186] Livy XXVI, 33, 10 (cf. IX, 16, 2).
[187] Id. IV, 50–51.
[188] Id. X, 9, 3–6.
[189] Id. III, 55, 4–5; Cic. *de re publica* II, 54.
[190] See pp. 22– 3 above.
[191] Livy X, 9, 4.
[192] Cic. *pro Rab. perd. reo*, 12; *in Cat.* IV, 10; Plut. *C. Gracchus*, 4.
[193] *Digest* 48.6.7; *Pauli Sententiae* V, 26, 1.
[194] See note 70 above.
[195] Referred to in the passages cited in note 70 above, and also Cic. *de domo* 43.
[196] Cic. *de re publica* II, 54.
[197] Livy II, 8, 2; Aristotle *Ath. Pol.* 9, 1; Polybius V, 27, 5–6.
[198] Livy II, 35, 2–6; Dion. Hal. VII, 38 ff., esp. 58.
[199] Livy II, 52, 3–5; 54, 2 ff.; 61; III, 31, 5–6.
[200] Livy III, 11, 6–13; Dion. Hal. X, 5–8.
[201] Livy III, 24, 3–8; 25, 1–3; 29, 6.
[202] Id. II, 41, 10–12; Cic. *de re publica* II, 60; Val. Max. V, viii, 2; VI, iii, 1 b.
[203] Tac. *Ann.* XI, 22, 3 f.
[204] *Digest* 1.13.1 pr.
[205] Zonaras VII, 13, 3 (see Cassius Dio, ed. Boissevain, I, pp. 40–41); Plutarch, *Publicola* 12 also dates the quaestors from 509 but makes them originally financial.
[206] Varro, *L.L.* V, 81.
[207] Festus, pp. 247, 310 Lindsay.
[208] *Digest* 1.2.2. 22–3.
[209] See note 202 above.
[210] See note 201 above.
[211] See note 180 above.
[212] See note 30 above.
[213] Varro, *L.L.* VI, 90.
[214] Livy I, 26.

[215] Festus, p. 380 Lindsay.

[216] Livy VI, 20, 12.

[217] Cassius Dio XXXVII, 27, 2.

[218] Livy III, 55, 6–10; Dion. Hal. VI, 89; Festus, p. 424 Lindsay.

[219] Pliny, *N.H.* VII, 143; Cic. *de domo* 123; Livy, *Per.* 59.

[220] Dion. Hal. VII, 21–66.

[221] Livy III, 55, 8–10.

[222] Id. III, 31, 5.

[223] Except that Dion. Hal. V, 19 includes fines under the first *lex Valeria.*

[224] Dion. Hal. X, 50; Cic. *de re publica* II, 60.

[225] Aulus Gellius, *N.A.* XI, 1, 4. Pliny, *N.H.* XVIII, 11 and XXXIII, 7 recalls fines in cattle.

[226] Two laws of commutation are recorded: a *lex Menenia Sestia* of 452 (Festus, pp. 268, 270 Lindsay, though muddled) and a *lex Iulia Papiria* of 430 (Cic. *de re publica* II, 60; Livy IV, 30, 3; Festus, p. 220 Lindsay).

[227] Cicero carefully distinguishes *iudicare* and *irrogare* in *de domo* 45, 'ante . . . quam multam irroget aut iudicet' and *de legibus* III, 6, 'cum magistratus iudicassit inrogassitve per populum multae poenae certatio esto'. Strictly speaking, *multam irrogare* should be used of comitial fines (as in Cic. *pro Rab. perd. reo* 8; *pro Milone* 36; *de domo* 58; Livy XXXVII, 58, 1; Asconius, p. 21) and *multam dicere* for fines inflicted by a magistrate within the legal limit (as in Aulus Gellius, *N.A.* XI, 1, 4, etc.). *Multam dicere* is, however, often loosely used for comitial fines (as in Cic. *Phil.* XI, 18; Livy XXV, 3, 13; XL, 42, 9, etc.), and *irrogare* more rarely for inflicting any penalty (*Bell. Afr.* 97, if *irrogatis* is correct). *Irrogare* is also used for *privilegia*, which were on my view analogous to comitial fines (as in Cic. *de domo* 43 and 110; *pro Sestio* 65; *de legibus* III, 11).

[228] Aulus Gellius, *N.A.* XX, 1, 7–8; Gaius, *Institutes* III, 189.

[229] See note 108 above; it was an offence under the Twelve Tables, Pliny, *N.H.* XXVIII, 17–18.

[230] Aulus Gellius, *N.A.* XX, 1, 7; *Digest* 47.9.9; Pliny, *N.H.* XVIII, 12.

[231] *F.I.R.A.* I, pp. 13–14 (=Servius' commentary on Virgil's *Eclogues*, 4, 43).

[232] Dion. Hal. X, 7.

[233] Cic. *de re publica* II, 54.

[234] Val. Max. VIII, i, absol. 1.

[235] See notes 214, 215 above.

NOTES TO CHAPTER 2

[1] Cic. *II in Verrem* I, 155–6.
[2] *Lex Latina tabulae Bantinae*, *F.I.R.A.* I, 6, §2. See note 51 below.
[3] *F.I.R.A.* I, 9, fragment C, ll. 18 ff.
[4] *F.I.R.A.* I, 12, §5.
[5] See pp. 82–3 below.
[6] *Digest* 3.3.42.1, and see p. 56 below.
[7] Justinian, *Institutes* 4.18.1.
[8] See, e.g., the *actio de sepulchro violato*, *Digest* 47.12.3 pr., and the *actio de deiectis et effusis*, *Digest* 9.3, esp. frag. 5.5.
[9] *Digest* 2.1.7 pr.
[10] Women and minors, who were normally excluded from making an accusation, were allowed to do so for the murder of a close relative or dependant, *Digest* 48.2.2.
[11] Cic. *in Vatinium* 27–8 and 33; *Schol. Bob.* p. 150 (Stangl).
[12] *F.I.R.A.* I, 7, ll. 11 and 13. It is assumed throughout this study that this text, the law of the Naples tablet, is the *lex Acilia repetundarum*, mentioned only by Cicero, *I in Verrem* 51. It will be very frequently quoted as such.
[13] Ib. l. 23.
[14] Livy XLIII, 2.
[15] Val. Max. VI, ix, 10; Livy, *Per.* 47 fin.
[16] Cic. *Brutus* 106; *de officiis* II, 75; *II in Verr.* III, 195; IV, 56.
[17] *F.I.R.A.* I, 7, ll. 23 and 58–9.
[18] Ib. ll. 12 ff.
[19] Plut. *C. Gracchus* 5 and *compar.* 2.
[20] Livy, *Per.* 60.
[21] Velleius II, 6, 3; 13, 2; 32, 3; Tac. *Ann.* XII, 60; Diodorus XXXIV–V, 25; Appian, B.C. I, 22, 2.
[22] See note 12 above.
[23] *F.I.R.A.* I, 7, ll. 12–14, 15–17.
[24] See the Appendix to this chapter.
[25] See *Proc. Cambridge Philological Soc.* 1960, pp. 39–42.
[26] 'Praetor qui hac lege quaeret', 'praetoris quaestio esto', 'praetor quoius ex hac lege quaestio erit', *F.I.R.A.* I, 7, passim.
[27] Ib. ll. 3, 4 etc.
[28] Ib. ll. 30–35.
[29] Ib. l. 57.
[30] Ib. ll. 1–3.
[31] Ib. ll. 59–61.
[32] Theft was a private law offence, a tort; but its penalty was normally double, sometimes treble or quadruple. And the 'lites quae infitiando crescunt in duplum' are numerous and well-known.

[33] Sallust, *Ep. ad Caesarem* II, 7, 12.

[34] Cic. *pro Cluentio* 148; 151; 154.

[35] *Digest* 48.8.1 pr. and 1; *Collatio leg. Mos. et Rom.* I, 2, 1; VIII, 4, 1 (cf. 7, 2) (=*F.I.R.A.* II, pp. 544 and 564–5).

[36] See Chapter 1, note 192. This law did not set up a *publicum iudicium* to secure its own enforcement: Popilius Laenas and later Opimius were tried by tribunes before the people (Cic. *de domo* 82; *de legibus* III, 26; Velleius II, 7, 3; Livy *Per.* 61; Cic. *de oratore* II, 106; 132). It is unlikely therefore that the law 'ne quis iudicio' established a *quaestio*.

[37] Cic. *pro Cluentio* 116; *I in Verrem* 38. In 72 B.C. Septimius Scaevola, who was alleged to have taken a bribe to condemn Oppianicus, was convicted *de repetundis*, and the jury conducting the *litis aestimatio* included this bribe in the sum they arrived at. If that *litis aestimatio* had counted as a judgment on those facts, says Cicero, Scaevola could have subsequently been tried 'hac ipsa lege', under the law under which Cluentius was being tried, i.e. the section of the *lex Cornelia de sicariis* which incorporated Gracchus' law.

[38] Plutarch, *Marius* 5; Val. Max. VI, ix, 14.

[39] Livy XL, 19 fin., 'leges de ambitu'; *Per.* 47; cf. Polyb. VI, 56, 4.

[40] Asconius, pp. 45–6; Cic. *de natura deorum* III, 74; Val. Max. III, vii, 9; VI, viii, 1.

[41] Sall. *Jugurtha* 40; Cic. *Brutus*, 128.

[42] Cic. *de inventione* I, 92.

[43] See Balsdon in *Papers of the British School at Rome* 1938, pp. 103 ff., whose argument has not been bettered. Only Tacitus, *Ann.* XII, 60 speaks explicitly of wholly senatorial juries.

[44] For the date of Glaucia's law see Balsdon, op. cit., pp. 106–8. For the date of his tribunate see Broughton, *Magistrates* I, pp. 571–3; but he could have passed the law as praetor in 100. Equestrian jurors are implied in Cic. *Brutus* 224 and explicitly mentioned in the passage from *pro Scauro* quoted by Asconius, p. 21.

[45] Cic. *pro Rabirio Postumo* 8–9.

[46] Cic. *pro Balbo* 54.

[47] Cic. *II in Verr.* I, 26. See below, p. 71.

[48] The persons qualified to bring a charge are enumerated in *F.I.R.A.* I, 7, ll. 1–3. A charge might be made 'alieno nomine' (l. 6), presumably by a procurator of the injured party. The reward for a successful prosecution is given to that one of the prosecutors who has contributed most to the condemnation (ll. 76 and 78).

[49] Cic. *div. in Caec.* 69, with the Pseudo-Asconius scholiast, Stangl p. 204; Appian, B.C. I, 22; *Mith.* 57.

[49a] Cic. *div. in Caec.* 63, with the scholiast, Stangl p. 203. For the dates see Broughton, *Magistrates* II, p. 18; I, p. 568; I, pp. 560, 562. I have brought down the case of Albucius; the date rests on a very tenuous argument. Pompeius must have been urban quaestor when he conducted the murder trial mentioned in chapter 1, p. 5 above (with note 31), and have served under Albucius in Sardinia *pro quaestore*.

[50] The reason for dating the *lex Appuleia* to 103 is that the offences for which Norbanus was tried under it occurred in that year. It is, however, possible that the law was later and retrospective, seeing that it merely redefined what had hitherto been called *perduellio*; the consuls of 132 were tried in 123 under Gaius Gracchus' law of that year which forbade capital trials without the people's consent. Saturninus' second tribunate in 100 would make the sequence of events more natural: Glaucia makes the jurors equestrian in the only existing *quaestio* in 101 (or 100, see note 44 above) and Saturninus follows suit in his new *quaestio*, or the two act simultaneously. If the Latin law of Bantia is part of the *lex Appuleia de maiestate* (see the next note below) there is a further indication for 100 B.C.: Appian, B.C. I, 29, implies that the clause in the *lex agraria* of Saturninus which imposed an oath to obey it on all senators was a novelty; the law of Bantia, which prescribes such an oath, should therefore not be earlier. For the content of the *lex Appuleia* see Cic. *de oratore* II, 107.

[51] Val. Max. VIII, v, 2; Cic. *de oratore* II, 198–9. The Latin law of Bantia (*F.I.R.A.* I, 6) is generally agreed to fall in this period because of the oath clause. It speaks in §2 of a '[ioudex] quei ex hace lege plebeive scito factus erit', and in §3 of a 'ioudex ex hace lege plebeive scito [factus]' existing in the future. It must therefore be a

law creating a new court, and not either of the *leges Serviliae*, for there was already a *praetor repetundarum*. It might be the law establishing a murder court or the court for *peculatus*, but the heavy penal clauses on magistrates and senators who fail to enforce it or to take the oath suggest something of high political importance, which would best fit *maiestas*.

[52] Cic. *Phil.* I, 21.

[53] See Chapter I above, pp. 28–9, with notes 162 and 167.

[54] Asconius, p 45.

[55] See Chapter I above, pp. 5–6, with note 31, and note 49a of the present chapter.

[56] Cic. *pro Roscio Amerino* 11 and 64. Fannius, the praetor *de sicariis* under whom Roscius was tried, had previously been *iudex quaestionis* of the same court.

[57] *I.L.S.* 45; Broughton, *Magistrates* II, pp. 1 and 3.

[58] Plut. *Pompey* 4.

[59] Appian, B C. I, 35; Livy, *Per.* 71; cf. Velleius II, 13, 2 and the *de viris illustribus* 66, 4 (transfer entirely to the senate).

[60] Cic. *pro Cluentio* 153; *pro Rab. Post.* 16.

[61] Appian, B.C. I, 37; Asconius, pp. 22 and 73–4; Val. Max. VIII, vi, 4; Cic. *Brutus* 304.

[62] Asconius, p. 79.

[63] The *leges Corneliae*: *de maiestate*, Cic. *in Pisonem* 50; *de repetundis*, Cic. *pro Rab. Post.* 9; *de sicariis*, Cic. *pro Cluentio* 148, 151, 154, *Digest* 48.8, passim, *Collatio leg. Mos. et Rom.* I, 1, 2 and 3 (*F.I.R.A.* II, p. 544), *Pauli Sententiae* V, 23 (*F.I.R.A.* II, pp. 408–410); *de ambitu*, *Schol. Bob.* p. 78 at bottom (Stangl); *testamentaria nummaria*, Cic. *II in Verr.* I, 108, *Digest* 48.10, passim (called *de falsis*), *Pauli Sententiae* V, 25. There is no formal proof of a *lex Cornelia de peculatu*, but the *quaestio* is attested in Cic. *pro Cluentio* 147 and *pro Murena* 42, and it is likely that in this case also Sulla re-enacted the earlier law. On the *lex Cornelia de iniuriis*: *Digest* 3.3.42.1 and 47.10. 5 pr., *Pauli Sententiae* V, 4, 8. On Sullan juries: Cic. *I in Verr.* 37, Velleius II, 32, Tac. *Ann.* XI, 22.

[64] Asconius, pp. 17, 67, 68, also pp. 53, 55; *Schol. Bob.* pp. 91, 94 (Stangl); Cic. *ad Att.* I, 16, 3. According to Livy, *Per.* 97, Plut. *Pompey* 22, the courts were transferred to the *equites*, according to Velleius II, 32, Cic. *pro Cluentio* 130 they were shared between *equites* and senate. In *pro Fonteio* 36, *pro Cluentio* 121, *pro Flacco* 96, *pro Rabirio Postumo* 14 Cicero mentions only senators and *equites*. In *pro Flacco* 4 there are fifty equestrian jurors. On *tribuni aerarii* see also the Appendix to this chapter.

[65] Asconius, p. 17, cf. Cic. *Phil.* I, 20; *in Pisonem* 94, and see p. 88 below.

[66] Asconius, pp. 38–9, cf. 53–5, and see p. 58 below.

[67] Suet. *div. Iul.* 41, 2; Cassius Dio XLIII, 25.

[68] Cic. *pro Caelio*, 70.

[69] Sall. *Cat.* 31, 4; Cic. *ad fam.* VIII, 8, 1; Asconius, p. 55. The two laws are usually assumed somehow to have been one (see, e.g. Mommsen, *Strafrecht*, p. 654, n. 2). This cannot be right.

[70] Cic. *Phil.* I, 23; *Digest* 48.6 and 7; *Pauli Sententiae* V, 26.

[71] Cic. *pro Murena* 46, 67; Asconius, pp. 69, 88; Cassius Dio XXXVI, 38–9 for the Sullan penalty.

[72] Cic. *pro Murena* 3, 5, 67, 89; *pro Sestio* 133; *in Vatinium* 37; *pro Plancio* 83; Cassius Dio XXXVII, 29, 1.

[73] Cic. *pro Plancio* 36–41; *ad fam.* VIII, 2, 1; *ad Att.* IV, 15, 9; Cassius Dio XXXIX, 37, 1; and see below p. 67.

[74] Asconius, p. 36; Caesar, B.C. III, 1; Appian, B.C. II, 23–4; Plut. *Cato minor* 48. Cic. *ad Att.* X, 4, 8 and Tac. *Dial.* 38 may be referring to this law or to the *lex Pompeia de vi*. We are not told on what charge Sestius was to be tried 'lege Pompeia' in Cic. *ad Att.* XIII, 49, 1, but it cannot have been *vis* and is unlikely to have been parricide, so it was probably *ambitus*.

[75] *lex Iulia de repetundis*: Cic. *pro Sest.* 135; *in Vatinium* 29; *pro Rab. Post*, 8, 12; *in Pisonem* 37, 50, 90; *de prov. cons.* 7; *de domo* 23; *ad fam.* II, 17, 2; V, 20, 2; *ad Att.* V, 10, 2 and 16, 3; *Digest* 48.11; *Pauli Sententiae* V, 28. *lex Iulia maiestatis*: Cic. *Phil.* I, 21–3; *Digest* 48.4; *Pauli Sententiae* V, 29.

[76] *Digest* 48.9, esp. frag. 9; *Pauli Sententiae* V, 24.

[77] Cic. *ad fam.* VIII, 12, 3 and 14, 4.

[78] Cic. *pro Rab. perd. reo* 8; *Digest* 48.15; *Pauli Sententiae* V, 30; *Collatio leg. Mos. et Rom.* XIV, 2 and 3.

[79] *lex Licinia Mucia*: Cic. *pro Balbo* 48; *lex Papia*: Cic. *pro Balbo* 52; *ad Att.* IV, 18, 4; *de lege agraria* I, 13; *pro Archia* 10; *de officiis* III, 47; Val. Max. III, iv, 5; Cassius Dio XXXVII, 9, 5.

[80] Cic. *ad Att.* I, 14, 2 and 5; 16, 2 ff.

[81] Asconius, pp. 38–9 and 53–5; Cic. *ad Att.* VIII, 16, 2; Velleius II, 76; Plut. *Pompey*, 55.

[82] *F.I.R.A.* I, 7, ll. 4, 6, 8, etc.

[83] Ib. I, 6, ll. 7–8 and 16–17.

[84] Cic. *pro Roscio Amerino* 11; he had previously been *iudex quaestionis* of the same court.

[85] Cic. *pro Cluentio* 147.

[86] C. Claudius Pulcher, c. 98 B.C.: *I.L.S.* 45, aed. cur., iudex q. veneficis, pr. repetundis. Antistius, 86 B.C.: Plut. *Pompey* 4 (who calls him praetor, but according to Velleius II, 26 he died *aedilicius*). M. Fannius, c. 82 B.C.: Cic. *pro Roscio Amerino* 11, praetor, previously *iudex quaestionis de sicariis*. C. Iunius, 74 B.C.: Cic. *pro Cluentio* 79, *aedilicius*. M. Plaetorius and C. Flaminius, 66 B.C.: Cic. *pro Cluentio* 126, 147, aediles, *iudices quaestionis de sicariis*. Julius Caesar, 64 B.C.: Suet. *div. Iul.* 11, after his aedileship. C. Octavius, c. 63 B.C.: *I.L.S.* 47, aed. pl. cum C. Toranio, iudex quaestionum, pr. Crassus Dives, 59 B.C.: Cic. *ad Att.* II, 24, 4, president of court *de vi*, then praetor in 57, Cic. *post red. in sen.* 22–3. C. Visellius Varro, c. 58 B.C.: Cic. *Brutus* 264, post curulem aedilitatem iudex quaestionis. Cn. Domitius, 56 B.C.: Cic. *pro Caelio* 32 and 70–72, presided over the first trial of Caelius *de vi*, and—if it is the same man—presided as praetor over his second trial in 54, Cic. *ad Quintum fratrem* II, 11, 2 (see note 89 below). M. Favonius, 52 B.C.: Plut. *Cato minor* 46; Cassius Dio XL, 45, 4, aedile in 53; Asconius, p. 54, *quaesitor de sodaliciis* in 52. C. Papirius Masso, ?late Republic: *I.L.S.* 907, aed. pl., q. iud. Other *iudices quaestionum* include Q. Curtius, 70 B.C.: Cic. *II in Verr.* I, 158; Q. Voconius Naso, 66 B.C.: Cic. *pro Cluentio* 148; L. Fabius and C. Considius, 52 B.C.: Asconius, pp. 54–5. It seems likely that Novius Niger, who was charged with receiving information laid against the Catilinarian conspirators in 62, Suet. *div. Iul.* 17, 1, was (as Suetonius says) a quaestor and not a *quaesitor*. The senior *quaesitores* of *vis* and *ambitus* under the *leges Pompeiae* of 52, Domitius Ahenobarbus and A. Torquatus, were special cases.

[87] For lots drawn by praetors elect: Cic. *I in Verrem*, 21; by *iudices quaestionum: Collatio leg. Mos. et Rom.* I, 3, 1. Of the presidents of courts in 66 B.C. mentioned in *pro Cluentio* 147 those of *ambitus*, *maiestas*, *repetundae* and *peculatus* were praetors, while the three presidents of *de sicariis et veneficis* were all *iudices quaestionum*. Of the *quaesitores* listed in note 86 above seven are *de veneficis*, four *de vi*, one (pre-Sullan) *peculatus*, one *de sodaliciis*, the rest unknown. Praetors so far as we know presided in the courts of *repetundae* (ten cases), *maiestas* (three cases), *ambitus* (two cases). They are found in charge of *peculatus* (twice), *sodalicia* (twice) and the court under *lex Papia* (once). There is only one case of a praetor presiding over the court for murder: Fannius in 80 B.C., when they still had only six courts for six praetors.

[88] Suet. *div. Iul.* 11; Cic. *pro Cluentio* 91–2, 96; *II in Verrem* I, 157–8; *pro Cluentio* 147; *Digest* 48.8.1.1.

[89] Scaurus *de vi*: Cic. *pro Sestio* 101, 116—he was governor of Sardinia next year, Asconius, p. 18. Cn. Domitius *de vi*: Cic. *pro Caelio* 32—his court was under the *lex Lutatia*, ib. 70–72. Cn. Domitius, *praetor ambitus*: Cic. *ad Quintum fratrem* II, 3, 6. Domitius *de vi*: ib. II, 11, 2.

[90] Asconius, pp. 54–5.

[91] Servilius: Cic. *ad Att.* IV, 15, 9 and 18, 4; *ad Quintum fratrem* III, 4, 6; Alfius: Cic. *pro Plancio* 43 (*de sodaliciis*); *ad Quintum fratrem* III, 1, 24 and 3, 3 (*de maiestate*); he is called *quaesitor* in both cases, but could have been praetor, as he had competed unsuccessfully for the praetorship of 55, Cic. *pro Sestio* 113–4 with *in Vatinium* 38. Cicero uses *quaesitor* of the praetor of a court, *I in Verr.* 29.

[92] See the Appendix to this chapter.

[93] *F.I.R.A.* I, 7, ll. 12–18.

[94] Cic. *pro Cluentio*, 121.

[95] Cic. *II in Verrem* I, 158; II, 79; *pro Cluentio* 103.

[96] The term *decuria* seems first to appear in this sense in Cic. *Phil.* I, 20.

[97] Cic. *ad fam.* VIII, 8, 5.

[98] Pliny, *N.H.* XXXIII, 31; *Tabula Hebana* (=Ehrenberg and Jones, *Documents illustrating the Reigns of Augustus and Tiberius*, 2nd ed., no. 94a), ll. 13–16.

[99] Cic. *pro Cluentio* 120.

[100] Cic. *in Pisonem* 94.

[101] See the previous note and Asconius, p. 17.

[102] See note 81 above.

[103] Suet. *div. Iul.* 41, 2; Cic. *Phil.* I, 20.

[104] See pp. 53–4 above.

[105] Cic. *ad fam.* VIII, 8, 2.

[106] Cic. *pro Balbo* 32, 52, 38.

[107] Cic. *pro Cluentio* 120.

[108] *Digest* 48.2, particularly fragments 1, 2, 4, 8, 9 and 11.

[109] Asconius, p. 54.

[110] Cic. *div. in Caec.* 24 and 68; *II in Verr.* II, 21–2; Pseudo-Asconius (Stangl), p. 194.

[111] Asconius, p. 21.

[112] Cic. *ad fam.* VIII, 8, 1.

[113] Cic. *pro Cluentio* 98.

[114] *F.I.R.A.* I, 7, ll. 3–4, 9, 19ff.

[115] Cic. *div. in Caec.* 64.

[116] Suet. *div. Iul.* 11.

[117] Cassius Dio XXXIX, 7; cf. Aemilius Scaurus (and his father) in Asconius, p. 19.

[118] Cic. *ad Att.* IV, 15, 9.

[119] Val. Max. III, vii, 9 (which provides the *terminus post quem* for the *lex Memmia*). The story is, however, odd, because one would have expected Antonius to be immune from prosecution as a magistrate in office. Perhaps the *lex Peducaea* under which he was accused had no clause exempting magistrates, so that he could only have pleaded the *lex Memmia*, which excused 'qui eorum rei p. causa abessent'.

[120] Cicero's *divinatio in Caecilium* is the only surviving speech at a *divinatio*, but he cites several cases in §§63–4. For the jury, see *II in Verr.* I, 15 and for the procedure Pseudo-Asconius (Stangl) p. 186—from which, and from Aulus Gellius, *N.A.* II, 4, it appears that the name of the process puzzled antiquaries. See also Cic. *ad fam.* VIII, 8, 3; *ad Quintum fratrem* III, 2, 1; Asconius, p. 39.

[121] Cic. *div. in Caec.* 69; *pro Fonteio* 36; *pro Flacco* 82; Asconius, pp. 38, 54, 59 (one *subscriptor*), Cic. *div. in Caec.* 47–9; Asconius, pp. 54–5; Val. Max. IV, ii, 5 (two), Cic. *pro Murena* 56; *ad Quintum fratrem* III, 3, 2; Asconius, p. 19 (three). A fourth is envisaged in Cic. *div. in Caec.* 49. None at all in Cic *ad fam.* VIII, 8, 1; Asconius p. 39. For an application to be *subscriptor* only see Cic. *div. in Caec.* 49, and for an accuser assigned as *subscriptor* Cic. *II in Verrem* I, 15.

[122] Cic. *div. in Caec.* 10–11 and 64–5 (citing another case, the choice of Piso by the Achaeans).

[123] See Chapter 3 below, p. 112 and nn. 153 and 154.

[124] Cic. *ad fam.* VIII, 8, 2.

[125] Asconius, p. 20.

[126] *Digest* 48.2.3 pr.

[127] Cic. *I in Verr.* 56 (in a rhetorical dress in *div. in Caec.* 19); Pseudo-Asconius (Stangl), p. 207; Asconius, p. 55.

[128] *F.I.R.A.* I, 7, l. 19; cf. oaths in private law actions, Gaius, *Institutes* IV, 172 and 176; *Digest* 39.2.7 pr.

[129] *Digest* 48.2.7.1.

[130] The test is the case of Sthenius in Cic. *II in Verrem* II, 94ff. The senate held it wrong to *recipere nomen* or *reum facere* in absence even in a provincial case (95), and Verres by claiming that it was legitimate in the provinces tacitly admitted that it was illegal at Rome (101).

131 Asconius, pp. 38–9 and 54. Asconius says that Milo 'postero die factus reus ambitus apud Manlium Torquatum absens damnatus est', which should mean that his name was received and he was condemned on the same day; but this must be a technical error: his name must have been received when he was ordered to be present and made his excuses.

132 Cic. *ad Att.* II, 24, 3–4.

133 Pseudo-Asconius (Stangl), p. 207: 'si tacuisset lis ei aestimabatur ut victo'.

134 *F.I.R.A.* I, 7, ll. 30–35.

135 Ib. I, 12, v; 21, xcv; 67, l. 66. Cf. also the *senatus consultum Calvisianum*, ib. 68, ll. 139–40.

136 Witnesses: Cic. *II in Verrem* II, 64–5. Documents: ib. II, 182, 186ff.; IV, 140, 149.

137 Asconius, p. 59 (*maiestas*); Plut. *Cicero* 9, 5 (*repetundae*).

138 *Inquisitio* is normally mentioned only in trials for *repetundae*, but it is envisaged for *ambitus* in Cic. *pro Murena* 44; and see the previous note for *maiestas*.

139 Scaurus: Asconius, p. 19. Cicero: Cic. *I in Verrem*, 6; *II in Verrem* I, 30 and II, 99.

140 Cic. *in Vatinium* 33.

141 P. 62 above, with note 111.

142 Cic. *I in Verrem* 6, *II in Verrem* I, 30.

143 *F.I.R.A.* I, 7, ll. 19ff., 30–32.

144 Cic. *I in Verrem* 16, 17, 31.

145 *F.I.R.A.* I, 7, ll. 20–26.

146 Cic. *pro Plancio* 41.

147 Id. *pro Sulla* 92.

148 See note 73 above.

149 Cic. *pro Roscio Amerino* 8.

150 Id. *I in Verrem* 16 and 30.

151 Id. *pro Cluentio* 91–2, 96, 103.

152 Id. *pro Cluentio* 91; *II in Verrem* I, 157–8; cf. *I in Verrem* 39.

153 Cassius Dio XXXIX, 7, 4; Cic. *ad Quintum fratrem* II, 1, 2 (where Watt reads not 'per praetorem urbanum' but 'per ⟨se⟩ praetor urbanus'); *ad Att.* IV, 3, 3; *ad Quintum fratrem* II, 3, 1 (Milo on trial, so Clodius now aedile).

154 Cic. *ad Quintum fratrem* II, 12, 2.

155 Id. *II in Verrem* II, 77.

156 Id. *I in Verrem* 29–30; *pro Cluentio* 74.

157 *F.I.R.A.* I, 7, l. 27.

158 Cic. *pro Cluentio* 103.

159 Id. *II in Verrem* I, 158.

160 Id. *pro Caecina* 28–9; *pro Cluentio* 103; *I in Verrem* 39.

161 Id. *pro Flacco* 4.

162 Id. *in Pisonem* 96.

163 Asconius, p. 28.

164 Cic. *ad Quintum fratrem* III, 4, 1.

165 Id. *ad Att.* IV, 15, 4.

166 Id. *ad Att.* I, 16, 5. But see p. 73 below.

167 See pp. 58 and note 81 above.

168 Cic. *II in Verrem* II, 99; Asconius, p. 60.

169 Asconius, p. 54 (Milo); p. 60 (Manilius).

170 *F.I.R.A.* I, 7, l. 29.

171 Criminal prosecutions: *Digest* 48, titles 1.6, 2.20, 16.15.3, 21.2–3; civil *actiones poenales*: Gaius, *Institutes* IV, 112 (the restriction to time before *litis contestatio* must be understood).

172 Val. Max. IX, xii, 7.

173 Plut. *Cicero* 9, 2; Cic. *ad Att.* I, 4, 2.

174 Cic. *II in Verrem* I, 26.

175 *F.I.R.A.* I, 7, ll. 46–8.

176 Cic. *II in Verrem* I, 26.

177 Evidence to come: Cic. *pro Rab. Post.* 31; *pro Sulla* 79; *pro Caelio* 63; evidence given: *pro Fonteio* 29; *pro Flacco* 10.

[178] Cic. *pro Flacco* 10, 51 and 31.

[179] Id. *pro Cluentio* 196; *II in Verrem* III, 74ff., esp. 89; and for the oath *pro Flacco* 17.

[180] Asconius, p. 28.

[181] Cic. *pro Roscio comoedo* 43–5; *pro Caelio* 55 (on oath); *pro Cluentio* 168 (in this case the witness was actually in court); Quintilian, *Inst. Or.* V, 7, 32 (*signatores* to depositions).

[182] *F.I.R.A.* I, 7, ll. 46–55.

[183] Cic. *pro Cluentio* 74–6, 106; *pro Caecina* 29.

[184] Id. *ad Att.* I, 16, 5 and 10; *Schol. Bob.* p. 91 (Stangl); Plut. *Cicero* 29, 6–8; *Caesar* 10, 11.

[185] Cic. *pro Cluentio* 55, 75.

[186] *F.I.R.A.* I, 7, l. 75.

[187] Caelius appears to allude to a vote of *calumnia*, Cic. *ad fam.* VIII, 8, 1.

[188] Cic. *de inventione* II, 59; *pro Sulla* 63 ('poena legis').

[189] Id. *pro Caecina* 100; and see p. 14 above, and p. 77 below.

[190] See p. 57 above, with note 72.

[191] Velleius II, 45, 1; Cic. *de domo* 47, 82.

[192] Cic. *Phil.* I, 23.

[193] There is no express statement of the *poena legis* for *maiestas* in the legal sources, but see *Pauli Sententiae* V, 29, 1: 'his antea in perpetuum aqua et igni interdicebatur'.

[194] *Pauli Sententiae* V, 23, 1; *Collatio leg. Mos. et Rom.* XII, 5, 1; *Digest* 48.8.3.5.

[195] *Pauli Sententiae* IV, 7, 1; *Digest* 48.10.33.

[196] *Digest* 48.13.3 ('in quam hodie successit deportatio').

[197] *Digest* 48.6.10.2; *Pauli Sententiae* V, 26, 1.

[198] *Digest* 48.7.1 pr.; *Pauli Sententiae* V, 26, 3.

[199] *Digest* 48.15.7.

[200] See notes 71 and 72 above.

[201] *F.I.R.A.* I, 7, ll. 58–9.

[202] Cic. *div. in Caec.* 19; *I in Verrem* 56.

[203] Id. *pro Cluentio* 116.

[204] *F.I.R.A.* I, 68, ll. 98–9.

[205] Suet. *div. Iul.* 43, 1; *Digest* 48.11.6.1.

[206] Cassius Dio, frag. 97, 1 (Boissevain, vol. I, pp. 338–9).

[207] E.g. *II in Verrem* III, 52, 129, 133–4.

[208] Cic. *pro Rab. Post.* 8–11.

[209] Id. *ad fam.* VIII, 8, 2–3.

[210] *F.I.R.A.* I, 7, ll. 69–72.

[211] See p. 47 above.

[212] Cic. *pro Caelio* 1; *I in Verrem* 31; cf. *ad fam.* VIII, 8, 5.

[213] *F.I.R.A.* I, 7, ll. 7–8.

[214] Cic. *ad Att.* I, 1, 2; cf. Suet. *div. Aug.* 32 fin., which probably means that Augustus stopped the holding of all trials in the last two months; there were many holidays in those months anyway.

[215] Verres hoped that his trial, which began on 5 August, would last into the new year (Cic. *I in Verrem* 31), and so did Sempronius Rufus (*ad fam.* VIII, 8, 1). Cicero received a charge against Manilius three days before his praetorship ran out (Plut. *Cicero* 9, 4).

[216] Cic. *de inventione* II, 58.

[217] Id. *pro Milone* 14.

[218] Id. *pro Cluentio* 56–9.

[219] See p. 62 above, with note 112.

[220] Asconius, p. 54.

[221] Sall. *Cat.* 51, 22.

[222] Cic. *pro Cluentio* 38–9.

[223] Val. Max. V, iv, 7 (already quoted, p. 15 above).

[224] *F.I.R.A.* I, 7, ll. 57–8.

[225] Cic. *pro Rab. Post.* 8.

[226] Strabo, p. 455 C, fin.

[227] See pp. 3–4 above.

[228] Appian, B.C. I, 22, 2.

229 Cic. *de oratore* I, 225; *Brutus* 164.
230 Livy, *Per.* 70; Velleius II, 13, 2.
231 *F.I.R.A.* I, 7, ll. 56–7, 73–4.
232 Asconius, pp. 38–9, 54–5; Cic. *pro Cluentio* 115–6.
233 Cic. *in Pisonem* 50.
234 See p. 25 above.
235 See Chapter 1, p. 5 above, with note 26.
236 Cic. *I in Verrem* 38.
237 Appian, B.C. I, 22, 6–7; 35, 5 ff.
238 Cic. *pro Rab. Post.* 16.
239 See p. 70 above.
240 See p. 51 above.
241 See note 37 above.
242 Cic. *pro Cluentio* 104; *Digest* 48.11, frags. 3, 6.2, 7 pr. At any rate in the Principate, people who bribed jurors could be tried under the *lex Cornelia de falsis*: *Digest* 48.10.1.1; *Pauli Sententiae* V, 25, 2.
243 Cic. *pro Cluentio* 144.
244 Id. *pro Rab. Post.* 14–18.
245 Ibid. 16–17.
246 Cic. *ad Atticum* I, 17, 8.
247 *Collatio leg. Mos. et Rom.* I, 3, 1.
248 The *Table of Heraclea*, *F.I.R.A.* I, 13, ll. 118–9.
249 Probably by *multae petitio*, as in the Law of Tarentum, *F.I.R.A.* I, 18, ll. 4–6.
250 Sex. Roscius of Ameria was killed at Rome: Cic. *pro Rosc. Am.* 18; the attempted murder of Cluentius of Larinum was at Rome: Cic. *pro Cluentio* 44ff.; and Oppianicus of Larinum was condemned—allegedly by a judicial conspiracy—at Rome: ib. 55ff. The only doubtful case is that of T. Caelius of Tarracina (Cic. *pro Rosc. Am.* 64).
251 Asconius, pp. 36, 38.
252 *F.I.R.A.* I, 19, xxi, l. 3 and xxii, l. 3; and (treating the *fragmentum Atestinum* as related to the *lex Rubria*) *F.I.R.A.* I, 20, l. 6.
253 Cic. *pro Cluentio* 147.
254 *F.I.R.A.* I, 18, ll. 4–6; 32–5.
255 Ib. 21, §§61, 74–5, 81–2, 125–6, 128–32, ad fin. in each case; and §95.
256 Ib. §§95, 102. These regulations certainly apply to *iudicia publica*: note in §95 the summons of witnesses by public authority and in §102 the terms characteristic of criminal law—*quaerere*, *delator*, *subscriptor*.
257 Cic. *II in Verrem* IV, 100.
258 Ib. II, 94, 98–9, 110; and see IV, 40; V, 109.
259 Ib. II, 94–5; 100–101.
260 Ib. I, 73–4.
261 Ib. V, 114.
262 Ib. II, 70.
263 Ib. V, 23.
264 Ib. I, 75.
265 Ib. II, 70–75
266 Ib. V, 158–62.
267 See Chapter 1, pp. 20–21 above, with note 132.

NOTES TO THE APPENDIX TO CHAPTER TWO

1 *Commentariolum Petitionis* 33.
2 *F.I.R.A.* I, 7, ll. 13 and 17; Suet. *div. Aug.* 32, 3 (reducing it again).
3 Cic. *de re publica* IV, 2.
4 Polybius VI, 20, 9; cf. Cic. *de re publica* II, 39; Livy V, 7, 5.
5 Horace, *Ep.* I, i, 58.
6 Pliny, *N.H.* XXXIII, 34.
7 Cic. *I in Verrem* 38; *pro Roscio comoedo*, 42.

[8] Cato in Aulus Gellius, *N.A.* VI, 10, 2 (but for 'Catonis' the editors prefer Lipsius' 'Varronis'); Varro, *L.L.* V, 181; Festus, p. 2 Lindsay.

[9] *Schol. Bob.*, p. 91 (Stangl).

[10] Asconius, p. 17.

[11] Cic. *Phil.* I, 20.

[12] Suet. *div. Aug.* 32, 3; *Calig.* 16, 2.

[13] Frontinus, *de aquaeductu* 101; Cassius Dio LV, 3, 2; Pliny, *Ep.* IV, 29.

[14] Pliny, *N.H.* XXXIII, 31.

[15] Suet. *div. Aug.* 32, 3.

[16] Pliny, *N.H.* XXXIII, 30.

[17] Tac. *Ann.* III, 30; Suet. *Tib.* 41.

[18] *I.L.S.* 6747; and cf. the 'equites omnium decuriarum quae iudiciorum publicorum causa constitutae sunt' of the *Tabula Hebana* (=Ehrenberg and Jones, *Documents illustrating the Reigns of Augustus and Tiberius*, 2nd ed., no. 94a), ll. 8 and 11.

[19] Pliny, *N.H.* XXXIII, 30.

[20] Seneca, *de beneficiis* III, 7, 7.

[21] *I.L.S.* 6523; 4093; 6772.

NOTES TO CHAPTER 3

[1] Suet. *div. Aug.* 34, 1; Cassius Dio LIV, 30, 4; *Digest* 48.5.

[2] Suet. *div. Aug.* 34, 1; 40, 2; Cassius Dio LIV, 16, 1; *Digest* 48.14.

[3] *Digest* 48.13.

[4] See pp. 88 fin.–90 above.

[5] Tac. *Ann.* III, 68.

[6] Ib. IV, 21; I, 72.

[7] Ovid, *Tristia* II, 131–2.

[8] Cassius Dio LIV, 3; Suet. *Tib.* 8.

[9] *F.I.R.A.* I, 68, ll. 97 ff.

[10] Cassius Dio LV, 7, 2.

[11] Suet. *div. Aug.* 33, 1 and 2; 51, 2.

[12] Cassius Dio LVI, 24, 7 (from *Exc. Val.*)

[13] Tac. *Ann.* III, 10; cf. 12 and II, 79.

[14] Ib. VI, 11.

[15] *Digest* 48.6.7; *Pauli Sententiae* V, 26, 1.

[16] Cassius Dio LIV, 10, 1.

[17] *Digest* 1.21.1 pr.

[18] Quintilian, *Inst. Or.* III, 10, 1.

[19] Tac. *Ann.* I, 74; II, 50; III, 22, 38, etc.

[20] Pliny, *Ep.* II, 11, 4; IV, 9, 17.

[21] See note 13 above, and cf. Tac. *Ann.* IV, 22.

[22] Tac. *Ann.* XIII, 10 and 32; XIV, 18; XVI, 9.

[23] Ib. I, 74; II, 27 ff.; III, 12–14, 38, 66–70; IV, 18–21, 28, 34–5; XI, 4; XII, 22, 52, 59, 65; XIII, 30, 43, 52; XIV, 18, 40, 46; XVI, 8, 30; Pliny, *Ep.* II, 11; III, 9; IV, 9. These are all for *repetundae* or *maiestas* or both; in Tac. *Ann.* XIII, 43 *peculatus* is one of the charges.

[24] Tac. *Ann.* I, 73; III, 49, 70; IV, 15, 31; VI, 8, 14; XI, 4; XIII, 30, 33; XIV, 28; XVI, 8; Suet. *Tib.* 30 (*praefectum alae*). These are all for *repetundae* or *maiestas* or both. In Tac. *Ann.* XIV, 40 two *equites* are tried in the senate for forgery as accomplices of senators.

[25] Tac. *Ann.* II, 42, 67; Cassius Dio LII, 43; LVII, 17, 4. By contrast the trials of Herod's sons and of Archelaus were held before the emperor: Josephus, *A.J.* XVI, 90–126; XVII, 344.

[26] Adultery: Tac. *Ann.* II, 50; III, 22–3; IV, 22, 42; VI, 47–8. Murder: ib. III, 12–14; IV, 22; XIII, 44. The last known murder trial in the senate is that of Herodes Atticus: Philostratus, *Vitae Soph.* II, 1, 8. Forgery: Tac. *Ann.* XIV, 40.

[27] Cassius Dio LXVII, 2; cf. LXVI, 19.

[28] Ib. LXVIII, 2 and 5; LXIX, 2; *S.H.A. M. Antoninus Phil.* 25, 6.

[29] Herodian II, 14, 3; Cassius Dio LXXIV, 2; *S.H.A. Severus* 7, 5.

[30] Cassius Dio LII, 31, 3.

[31] Tac. *Dialogus*, 7, 1.

[32] Pliny, *Ep.* VI, 31, 7–12.
[33] Tac. *Ann.* IV, 15; XIII, 33.
[34] Pliny, *Ep.* VI, 31, 4–6.
[35] Tac. *Ann.* XIII, 30.
[36] Suet. *div. Aug.* 51, 2.
[37] Pliny, *Ep.* VI, 31, 3.
[38] Ib. VII, 6, 8.
[39] See pp. 101–3 below.
[40] Dio LI, 19, 7. For the phrase see Philostratus, *Vitae Soph.* II, 3 (568).
[41] Tac. *Ann.* III, 51; Suet. *Tib.* 75; Cassius Dio LVII, 20.
[42] Suet. *Nero* 10, 2.
[43] Tac. *Ann.* III, 70; XIV, 48; XVI, 11; Suet. *Nero* 39, 2.
[44] Tac. *Ann.* VI, 5; XVI, 8.
[45] Cassius Dio LIX, 18.
[46] *Digest* 49.2.1.2.
[47] Tac. *Ann.* I, 75; Suet. *Tib.* 33; Cassius Dio LVII, 7.
[48] Tac. *Ann.* XIV, 41.
[49] *Digest* 48.14.1 pr.
[50] *Digest* 48.1.8.
[51] *I.L.S.* 1332.
[52] To the material in de Ruggiero, *Dizionario Epigrafico*, s.v. 'iudex' (1943, F. Bozza) add *L'année épigraphique* 1951, no. 181; 1966, no. 252. The latest seem to be *I.L.S.* 6616 of A.D. 205 (though the man concerned there is clearly old) and *C.I.L.* VIII, 1576, a dedication to divus Pertinax. *C.I.L.* VIII, 26624 may also be Commodan in date. Dr. R. P. Duncan-Jones kindly provided this information.
[53] Pliny, Ep. IV, 29, and see p. 89 above.
[54] *Digest* 1.12.1, pr. and 4, cf. Cassius Dio LII, 21, 1–2.
[55] Cassius Dio LII, 20, 5–21, 2.
[56] *Digest* 48.5.30.5; 48.2.16.
[57] *Digest* 1.21.1 pr.
[58] *Digest* 1.2.2.33; 1.15.3, 1 and 4.
[59] *Digest* 48.12.3.1.
[60] *Collatio leg. Mos. et Rom.* XIV, 3, 2.
[61] Pliny, *Ep.* VII, 6, 8.
[62] Cassius Dio LXIX, 18.
[63] *S.H.A. Severus*, 4, 3.
[64] See note 60 above.
[65] Philost. *Vitae Soph.* II, 32 fin.—the sophist Heliodorus.
[66] *Codex Iustinianus* 4.65.4.
[67] Ib. 8.40.13.
[68] *Pauli Sent.* V, 12, 6.
[69] *F.I.R.A.* I, 68, edict 1, passim.
[70] Ib. edict 4, ll. 4–5.
[71] Pliny, *Ep.* II, 11, 8.
[72] *Collatio leg. Mos. et Rom.* XIV, 3, 3.
[73] Cassius Dio. LXXVI, 16.
[74] Suet. *Galba* 9, 1.
[75] Pliny, *Ep.* X, 58.
[76] Cassius Dio, LI, 19.
[77] See A. H. M. Jones, *Studies in Roman Government and Law*, p. 191, notes 82–3.
[78] *Acta Apost.* 25, 6–12.
[79] Ib. 25, 27; 26, 29; 27, 1, etc.
[80] Pliny, *Ep.* X, 96, 3–4.
[81] Eusebius, *H.E.* V, 1 passim, esp. 44.
[82] *Digest* 28.3.6.9; 49.9.1; 49.5.2.
[83] Cassius Dio LIII, 13, 6–7.
[84] Ib. LII, 22, 2–5.
[85] *I.L.S.* 1368; 2770; 9200.
[86] *I.L.S.* 1111; 1356 (=*C.I.L.* VIII, 20996, cf. 20995, the same man); *I.G.R.R.* IV, 1057.

[87] *I.L.S.* 1372.
[88] Tac. *Ann.* I, 29.
[89] Ib. III, 21.
[90] Josephus, *B.J.* II, 117.
[91] Cf. *Acta Apost.* 10, 1.
[92] *Digest* 1.16.6; 1.18.6.8; 2.1.3.
[93] *Digest* 1.21.1.1; 1.21.5.1; 2.1.3.
[94] *Digest* 1.16, frags. 6 pr. and 11; 1.21.1. 1.
[95] *Digest* 1.16.11.
[96] *Passio S. Perpetuae*, 6.
[97] Cassius Dio LII, 22; *Pauli Sent.* V, 26, 2.
[98] *Digest* 28.3.6.9; 49.1.16.
[99] *Pauli Sent.* V, 35, 2.
[100] *Digest*, 48.19.15.
[101] *Digest* 48.22.6.2.
[102] See the *Digest* references in Jones, *Studies in Roman Government and Law*, p. 185, notes 28–9.
[103] Cassius Dio LII, 19, 2–3.
[104] Pliny, *Ep.* II, 11, 4; IV, 9, 17 (cf., already in Tiberius' day, Tac. *Ann.* III, 23; 49–51; IV, 30).
[105] Pliny, *Ep.* IV, 9, 6–8 and 16–18.
[106] *Digest* 1.16.6.3.
[107] *Digest* 48.8, frags. 3.4 and 6. This was probably following a ruling of Domitian: Suet. *Dom.* 7; Cassius Dio LXVII, 2; Ammianus Marcellinus XVIII, 4, 5. The *senatus consultum* is dated A.D. 97 by *Digest* 48.8.6.
[108] *Digest* 48.8.3, pr. to 4.
[109] Cic. *de inventione* II, 53.
[110] Cic. *in Pisonem* 50; *Digest* 48.4, frags. 1, 2, 3, 4 and 10.
[111] *Digest* 48.4.5.
[112] Tac. *Ann.* I, 73–4; III, 49, 70, etc.
[113] Ib. I, 72. A further extension of charges from libel to slander appears under Tiberius (ib. I, 74; II, 50, etc.) but probably goes back to Augustus, since Tacitus does not call attention to this extension of the law as an innovation of Tiberius.
[114] *Digest* 48.10.15 pr. Cf. 48.10, frag. 1.7–8, and frags. 5, 6, 10, 11, 14, the rest of 15, etc.
[115] *Digest* 48.10.32.1.
[116] Cic. *II in Verrem* V, 7.
[117] *Digest* 47.11, frags. 10 and 9 respectively.
[118] *Digest* 47.2.93.
[119] *Digest* 47, titles 17 and 18.
[120] *Abigei*: *Digest* 47.14; *Pauli Sent.* V, 18; *Collatio leg. Mos. et Rom.* XI, 2–8. *Receptatores*: *Digest* 47.16.
[121] *Iniuria*: *Digest* 47.11.1 pr. and 2; 47.11.4; *Pauli Sent.* V, 4, 4–5 and 8, 16, 17, 21. Wheat: *Digest* 47.11.6 pr. Tombs: *Digest* 47.12.11. Boundary stones: *Digest* 47.21; *Pauli Sent.* I, 16. Fortune telling and religions: *Pauli Sent.* V, 21. Christianity: the crucial proof that the profession of Christianity was a capital offence is in Pliny, *Ep.* X, 96.
[122] *Digest* 47.20.
[123] *Digest* 47.19, esp. frag. 1.
[124] Plain death: *Digest* 48.19.8.1. *Summa supplicia*: *Pauli Sent.* V, 17, 2. Impaling and burning: *Digest* 48.19, frags. 9.11; 28 pr. and 11–12 and 15; 8.2; 38.1; *Pauli Sent.* V, 24 and 29, 1. Condemnation to the *ludi*: *Digest* 48.19, frags. 8.11; 11.3; 12; 31 pr.; *Pauli Sent.* V, 19 and 24 and 29, 1.
[125] Mines: *Digest* 48.19, frags. 8.4ff.; 23; 28.6. *Servus poenae*: *Digest* 48.19, frags. 17; 8.12.
[126] *Digest* 48.19, frag. 8.7, with the implications of frag. 8.4 init.
[127] *Digest* 48.19.2.1.
[128] Cassius Dio LVI, 27, 2. Boissevain reads 'Samos' by conjecture for 'Sardinia'; see the *apparatus* ad loc.
[129] Tac. *Ann.* III, 68–9; IV, 21, 30.

[130] *Digest* 48.19.2.1; 48.22.6 and 14; 1.12.1.3.
[131] *Digest* 48.22, frags. 4; 7; 14; 18.
[132] *Digest* 48.22.7.20–22.
[133] *Digest* 48.19.9, pr.–8.
[134] *Digest* 48.19, frags. 7 and 28.3; 48.1.2 fin.; 48.7.1.
[135] No *Digest* title sets out the rules about *honestiores* and *humiliores* systematically. For some of the material see Mommsen, *Römisches Strafrecht*, pp. 1032–7 and G. Cardascia in *Revue historique de droit français et étranger*, 1950, pp. 305ff. and 461ff.
[136] Pliny, *Ep.* II, 11, 8.
[137] See note 100 above.
[138] *Digest* 47.21.2; *Collatio leg. Mos. et Rom.* XIII, 3.
[139] *Digest* 48.5.39.8 and 48.8.1.5.
[140] *Digest* 48.22.6.2.
[141] Suet. *div. Iul.* 42, 3.
[142] Cassius Dio LVI, 27, 3.
[143] Tac. *Ann.* III, 17, 23; IV, 20–21, etc.
[144] *Digest* 48.20, frags. 1 and 7.
[145] *Postulatio*: Tac. *Ann.* III, 10. *Subscribere*: ib. I, 74.
[146] Ib. II, 50.
[147] Pliny, *Ep.* II, 11, 10–18; IV, 9, 3–15.
[148] Tac. *Ann.* III, 23, 49–51; 68; Pliny, *Ep.* II, 11, 19–22; IV, 9, 16–19.
[149] Tac. *Ann.* I, 74.
[150] Ib. IV, 21.
[151] Ib. III, 19; IV, 20, 30; VI, 47, etc. Penalties: ib. VI, 30.
[152] *F.I.R.A.* I, 68, Edict V, passim.
[153] Pliny, *Ep.* II, 11, 2 and 19; III 4, 3; 9, 7 and 21 and 23; VI, 29, 7–11; X, 3a, 2.
[154] Ib. V, 20, 1; VII, 6, 1; VII, 10 ('the Bithynians'). In II, 11, 2 and X, 3a, 2 the phrases 'accusantibus Afris' and 'provinciales' are, however, misleading, since Marius Priscus was accused by 'una civitas publice multique privati', III, 9, 4. Tacitus uses similar vague phrases, which may denote the provincial *concilium*: *Ann.* III, 66; IV, 15; XIII, 33; XIV, 18, 28, 46.
[155] Pliny, *Ep.* IV, 9, 3; V, 20, 4.
[156] Ib. VII, 6, 3.
[157] Ib. V, 20, 1; VI, 29, 8; Tac. *Ann.* XIII, 43, 52.
[158] Pliny, *Ep.* V, 20, 2–7.
[159] Ib. II, 11.
[160] Ib. IV, 9.
[161] Tac. *Ann.* IV, 22.
[162] *Acta Alexandrinorum*, IV, *Acta Isidori*, ll. 25–7 (page 12 of the Teubner text).
[163] Pliny, *Ep.* VI, 31; IV, 22; VI, 22.
[164] *Codex Iustinianus* 9.51.1; Roussel and De Visscher in *Syria* XXIII (1942–3), pp. 173ff.
[165] *I.L.S.* 1423, 1455 (the *iurisperitus*).
[166] *F.I.R.A.* I, 59, ll. 23–5.
[167] *L'année épigraphique*, 1921, nos. 38–9.
[168] Pliny, *Ep.* X, 96.
[169] *Digest* 22.5.3, paras. 1 and 3 (including the emperor: 'nam ipsos interrogare soleo').
[170] *Acta Alexandrinorum* IV, *Acta Isidori*, ll. 43ff (page 13 of the Teubner Text); IX, *Acta Pauli et Antonini*, ll. 44ff. (page 38 of the Teubner text); XI, *Acta Appiani*, passim (pp. 51–6 of the Teubner text).
[171] *Digest* 22.5, frags. 1.2; 3.6.
[172] *Digest* 22.5, frags. 4, 5, 8, 9, 19; *Collatio leg. Mos. et Rom.* IX, 2, 3 and 3, 2–3; *Pauli Sent.* V, 15, 2–3.
[173] *Digest* 22.5, frags. 3.5; 13; 15 pr.; *Collatio leg. Mos. et Rom.* IX, 2, 2.
[174] *Digest* 22.5.3.1–2.
[175] *Digest* 22.5.3.3–4.
[176] *Digest* 48.18 passim. This did not begin with the Principate, of course.
[177] *Digest* 48.18.1.23.
[178] *Digest* 48.18.1, paras. 19, 22, 27.

[179] *Digest* 48.18.1.5–6 (and passim); Tac. *Ann.* II, 30; *Pauli Sent.* V, 16, 5–9.
[180] *Digest* 48.18, frags. 5; 6 pr.; 17 pr.
[181] *Codex Iustinianus* 9.41.1 pr. (adding fraud against the census).
[182] Cassius Dio LV, 5, 4; LVII, 19, 1b and 2; Tac. *Ann.* II, 30; III, 22, 67.
[183] *Digest* 48.5.28.11 ff.
[184] *Digest* 48.18.9.2.
[185] *Digest* 48.18.1.3, a daughter beloved by both her parents, produced by her father for the prosecution; 48.18.1.10, a brother against an accused brother.
[186] *Codex Iustinianus*, 9.41.11 pr.
[187] *Digest* 48.18, frags. 1.9; 15 pr.; 22.
[188] *Codex Iustinianus*, 9.41.11.1.
[189] Ib. 9.41.8 pr.
[190] See the examples in Mommsen, *Römisches Strafrecht*, p. 406, notes 3 and 4.
[191] *Digest* 48.18.10.1; *Pauli Sent.* V, 29, 2.
[192] *Digest* 48.18, frags. 1, pr. and 1 and 4; 8 pr.; *Pauli Sent.* V, 14, 1.
[193] *Digest* 1.18, frags. 3; 13 pr.
[194] See A. H. M. Jones, *The Greek City*, pp. 212–3.
[195] *Digest* 48.3.6.
[196] *Codex Iustinianus* 9.2.7; *Digest* 48.16.6.3.
[197] Pliny, *Ep.* X, 96, 5–6; 97, 2.
[198] All these details in *Digest* 48.2 passim and 48.4, frags. 7 and 8.
[199] *Digest* 48.2.18.
[200] *Digest* 48.2.16.
[201] *Digest* 48.2.7, pr. and 1; *Codex Iustinianus* 9.1.3.
[202] *Pauli Sent.* V, 16, 14.
[203] *Digest* 48.3, frags. 1 and 3.
[204] *Digest* 48.1.12.
[205] *Digest* 48.18.18.9.
[206] *Digest* 1.16.6 pr.
[207] *Digest* 48.3.10.
[208] *Digest* 48.17; *Codex Iustinianus* 9.2.6; 9.40.1
[209] *Codex Iustinianus* 9.2.4.
[210] *Digest* 48.16.1.7.
[211] *Digest* 48, titles 2.3.4; 11.2; 16.10.
[212] *Digest* 48, titles 2.20; 16.15.3.
[213] *Digest* 48.16.1.1–6.

INDEX